the california garden tour

the california garden tour

The 50 Best Gardens to Visit in the Golden State

DONALD OLSON

TIMBER PRESS
PORTLAND, OREGON

Timber Press
The Haseltine Building
133 S.W. Second Avenue, Suite 450
Portland, Oregon 97204-3527
timberpress.com

Printed in China
Text design by Matthew Enderlin based on a series design by Laken Wright
Cover design by Anna Eshelman based on a series design by Laken Wright

Library of Congress Cataloging-in-Publication Data

Names: Olson, Donald, 1950– author.
Title: The California garden tour: the 50 best gardens to visit in the
    Golden State / Donald Olson.
Description: Portland, Oregon: Timber Press, 2017. | Includes
    bibliographical references and index.
Identifiers: LCCN 2016055616 | ISBN 9781604697223 (pbk.)
Subjects: LCSH: Gardens—California—Guidebooks. |
    California—Guidebooks.
Classification: LCC SB466.U65 C27 2017 | DDC 635.09794—dc23 LC record
available at https://lccn.loc.gov/2016055616

ISBN-13: 978-1-60469-722-3
1. Gardens—California—Guidebooks. 2. California—Guidebooks. I. Title.
SB466.U65N767 2014
635.09795—dc23

2013043425

To the directors, docents, and dedicated volunteers who keep California's gardens alive and growing, I tip my hat, lower my sunglasses, and say "thank you."

Wisteria blossoms along a veranda overlooking the romantic gardens at Filoli, south of San Francisco.

contents

Echeveria agavoides 'Red Tip', tightly planted in a container at the Mendocino Coast Botanical Gardens.

introduction

"I firmly believe from what I have seen that it is the chosen spot of all this earth as far as Nature is concerned." Luther Burbank wrote those words in 1875. He had just arrived in California and could barely contain his excitement. The state's natural beauty, diverse plant life, and Mediterranean climate acted on this transplanted New Englander just as it has on millions of visitors since.

Of course, California is a very different place from what it was in Burbank's time. He arrived only twenty-five years after California had achieved statehood. It hadn't yet become the political, economic, and agricultural powerhouse it is today. Now, with a population of nearly 39 million people, California shares the same urban and environmental woes we all share, and a few that are unique to California alone. But California also has some of the greatest gardens you will ever see, anywhere. Period. And once you visit a few of them, you may find yourself texting, tweeting, or emailing your friends back home using the same exultant language that Burbank used in 1875.

A BRIEF HISTORY OF CALIFORNIA GARDENS

The fifty gardens I've included fall into four basic types: estate gardens (once private, now public), botanical gardens, parks, and art gardens. In each entry I describe the background or backstory of the garden, but it's also useful to have a historical overview of gardens and gardening in California as a whole.

Native Peoples

Dates vary, but it's safe to assume that California has been inhabited for at least 12,000 years and probably longer. The two primary native groups were the Tongva people, who lived in the south, roughly from the Los Angeles Basin to San Diego, and the Ohlones, who inhabited the San Francisco Peninsula down to Monterey. Although it's possible that there was some cultivation of plants, the two indigenous groups were primary hunter-gatherers who subsisted on game, fish, shellfish, and a seasonal harvest of acorns, berries, seeds, and roots. They also used native plants for basket weaving and dyes, and to make their shelters.

The magnificent collection of king palms at the Virginia Robinson Gardens in Beverly Hills is the largest outside of Australia.

The San Diego Botanic Garden's Native Plants and Native People Trail features a re-creation of the frond-roofed, dome-shaped dwellings of the Kumeyaay people, and shows the plants they used. The Native Basketry Garden at the Marin Art and Garden Center is a habitat garden created to show the kinds of plants native peoples used to fashion their baskets.

The Mission Era

Gardening in California began in the late eighteenth century with the establishment of Catholic missions by the Spanish Franciscan Order. Twenty-one missions were founded from San Diego to Monterey and as far north as San Francisco between 1789 and 1833. Their goal was to convert ("civilize") the Indians and further cement Spain's claims to Alta California (what is today California). The Franciscans had to become self-sufficient in short order and feed the Spanish military forces. To that end, they created farms and gardens at each of their mission outposts and began cultivating European fruits, grains, and vegetables.

To maintain their gardens and ranches (livestock was also raised), the missionaries basically enslaved the native populations and forced them to work in the fields. So, even as it introduced

agriculture to California, the mission system undermined and eventually helped to destroy a way of life that had existed for thousands of years.

Barley, maize, and wheat were the most common cereal crops grown at the missions. The Franciscans also planted the first stone fruit and citrus trees in California. These were grown from seeds brought from Europe. Their fruit crops eventually included apples, peaches, pears, figs, and oranges.

The first grapes in California—*criolla* or Mission grapes— were planted in 1779 at Mission San Juan Capistrano and used to make wine. The region's first citrus orchard was planted in 1804 at Mission San Gabriel Arcángel. Olives were first cultivated and pressed for their oil at Mission San Diego de Alcála. None of this could have happened without water. The Franciscans created the first irrigation systems in California, channeling water from rivers and streams to water crops, fill cisterns, and trickle from fountains. You can see a preserved portion of one of their aqueducts, built with Indian labor, at the Santa Barbara Botanic Garden.

The Native Plants and Native People Trail at the San Diego Botanic Garden takes visitors to a re-created Kumeyaay dwelling site.

Farming, yes, but what about gardens? The Franciscans were focused on food, but it seems more than likely that some prized and purely ornamental plants, vines, and trees made their way into protected courtyards and perhaps into graveyards. We can't know for sure, because although the missions have been restored—they are the oldest buildings in California—none of the mission gardens survived. The gardens you can see around the San Carlos Borromeo de Carmelo Mission in Carmel-by-the-Sea and the courtyard garden in Mission Santa Barbara are both recent, and don't necessarily reflect the original plant material or how it was cultivated. But if you visit Marin Art and Garden Center, you can pay your respects to a living descendant of the mission era: a pear tree grown from a graft taken from the last remaining pear tree in the orchard of Mission San Rafael.

Mexico Takes Control

In 1821, Mexico gained independence from Spain and took control of Alta California, but the Spanish missions remained in control of their vast land holdings for another twelve years. Following the passage of the Mexican secularization act in 1833, the missions were dissolved, their buildings and gardens abandoned, and mission lands were divided into land grants. The land grants were the basis for the establishment of huge ranches encompassing tens and even hundreds of thousands of acres. A few of the gardens in this book—Rancho Los Alamitos and the Marin Art and Garden Center are prime examples—occupy former land grant ranches.

On the ranches, small adobe homes were built and the land was used primarily for raising livestock. But, again, it's hard not to surmise that some of those adobes built during the Mexican era, at least the ones in Monterey, the capital of Alta California, did not have an ornamental plant or two. Since the days of Spanish control, Monterey had been the only port of entry into Alta California, and seeds and cuttings of plants probably arrived by ship from foreign ports.

The Golden Garden State

In 1848, following the Mexican-American War, the United States marched troops into Alta California and took control of land that had been claimed by Spain, won by Mexico, and would, in 1850, become America's thirty-first state. The gardenization of California was underway.

The discovery of gold at Sutter's Mill near Sacramento, and the ensuing Gold Rush, brought tens of thousands of immigrants from around the world to the new state of California. In the 1850s, San Francisco became a city (it had been a Mexican settlement called Yerba Buena) and the horticultural know-how of transplanted easterners and Europeans, combined with the wealth created by the Gold Rush, began to transform the community into a city of gardens.

After the Gold Rush came the Land Rush. In 1862, President Lincoln signed the Homestead Act, entitling male U.S. citizens to claim 160 acres of land; if they were married, they could claim an additional 160. The stipulation was that the land had to be "improved." Easterners and immigrants from all over the world began to claim land and settle throughout California.

Farmers, orchardists, fruit growers, and vintners began to plant the crops that would eventually turn California into the nation's agricultural giant. But San Francisco, because of its accumulation of wealth, became the center of a new world of horticulture. Plant nurseries flourished. New plants arrived by ship, later by train, from nurseries in the East and in Europe, and were imported from Australia, Central and South America, and other exotic locales. The grounds of city mansions and estates on the Peninsula were transformed as acacias, eucalyptus, fig, and palm trees were planted; rose

Beautiful old catch basin grates in the Conservatory of Flowers, Golden Gate Park, San Francisco.

bowers were established; and pelargoniums, fuchsias, begonias, camellias, lilies, and other ornamental plants proliferated.

None of those early San Francisco gardens remain, but Golden Gate Park certainly does. Surveying for the park got underway in 1870. The Picturesque style of landscaping (a naturalistic approach) created by Frederick Law Olmsted in New York's Central Park was the model for Golden Gate Park. The park's Conservatory of Flowers, erected in 1879, is the oldest public wood-and-glass conservatory in North America, and among the few buildings to survive the 1906 San Francisco earthquake. The first gardens on Alcatraz Island, back when it was an army fort and not a federal prison, were also planted before 1900.

Fairs and Expositions

World's fairs and expositions have disappeared from American life now, but in the late nineteenth and early twentieth centuries they were huge booster events that drew hundreds of thousands of people to California and introduced them to new plant materials, new garden styles, and a Mediterranean climate that provided seemingly endless possibilities for gardening—provided you had a water source. They were also a source of rivalry between San Francisco and San Diego.

The first big event was the California Midwinter International Exposition of 1894, held in San Francisco's still uncompleted Golden Gate Park. One of the exposition's most popular attractions was the Japanese Village exhibit, with its Japanese tea house and tea garden. It was the first time most people in California had seen an Asian-influenced garden, and it was such a hit that the garden remained as a permanent fixture when the exposition ended. The Japanese Garden in Golden Gate Park is now recognized as the oldest Japanese-style garden in the United States.

Although the land for Balboa Park—San Diego's answer to Golden Gate Park—was acquired in 1868, the creation of the park didn't really start until 1902. Work was spurred on when San Diego lost its bid to host the 1915 World's Fair to San Francisco and decided to hold a fair of its own: the Panama-California Exposition. The buildings erected for the event epitomize the Beaux-Arts style then in vogue. One notable veteran of the exposition is the Botanical Building, a remarkably attractive cast-iron conservatory sheathed with redwood and fronted by a rectangular lily pond. The Japanese Friendship Garden also dates from that time.

San Francisco, meanwhile, hosted the immensely successful Panama-Pacific International Exposition, a world's fair that left the city with several notable structures, including the Palace of the Legion of Honor and the San Francisco Ferry Building. The fair was meant to signal to the world that San Francisco had risen from the rubble of the 1906 earthquake and was ready to grow again. The fair's Japanese Pavilion had such a profound impact on San Francisco socialite and philanthropist Isabel Stine that in 1917 she created her own Japanese-style garden, called Hakone, about fifty miles south of San Francisco in Saratoga.

San Diego eventually did get a world's fair of its own: the California Pacific International Exposition of 1935. The park's Alcazar Garden, created for the fair, reflects the Hispano-Moorish (Spanish Colonial Revival) style that had become popular throughout California in the 1920s. I haven't been able to discover if the park area where professional nudists frolicked behind a fence for the titillation of fairgoers had a garden in it or not.

Beaux-Arts, Spanish Colonial Revival, and the Country Place Era

Starting in the early 1900s, as fortunes were made from railroads, oil, mining, and ranching, grand estates with lavish gardens began to appear on the Peninsula (propelled by an exodus from San Francisco after the 1906 earthquake), in Santa Barbara, and in Los Angeles. These locales were not the overbuilt, car-clogged places we see today. California was still rural, agricultural, and relatively undeveloped (although you could see oil derricks in Los Angeles). It was possible, if you were rich enough, to buy lots of land and transform it into your personal Eden.

Up until the 1940s, California mansions, villas, and gardens were typically built in an East Coast or European formal style supplemented by a vast assortment of exotic plant material. French-inspired Beaux-Arts was one style, Italian Mediterranean was another, but it was the Spanish Colonial Revival style with its patios and tiles—the style we now associate with California—that really caught hold. Moorish elements, in the form of geometrically shaped fountains, found their way into many gardens of the 1920s, along with imported palm trees and other semi-tropical plants.

The 1920s are part of a period referred to as the Country Place Era because many wealthy easterners and Californians built rural retreats during that time—retreats that, in most cases, became their permanent homes.

Plant collecting became a passion among wealthy Californians establishing new estates, and horticulturalists and landscape architects entered the gardening arena. William Hertrich, John McLaren, Kate Sessions, Florence Yoch, Lockwood de Forest, Jr., and Ralph Stevens are some of the garden designers and horticulturists you will meet in the pages of this book.

Seeds and cuttings of new plants were obtained by rich plant lovers on their world travels or from a network of botanical gardens, specialty nurseries, and other private estates. Except for trees, there wasn't much interest in utilizing local native plants in any of these gardens. The goal was to transform the landscape into something that reflected status by mimicking garden styles from the East Coast or Europe. This impression was possible because if you could obtain the plants, virtually anything would grow in California's Mediterranean climate—provided you had the right soil, drainage, and a source of water. Private estates had their own private sources of water in the form of streams, rivers, and aquifers.

The large-scale dam building that transformed California's water supply didn't begin until the 1920s.

Cacti and succulents were the exceptions when it came to using native California plants in gardens of this era. They were dug up from the Sonoran and Mojave Deserts (and from deserts in the Southwest, Mexico, and Central America) and used in gardens throughout fast-growing Southern California. It was this whole-sale destruction of California's desert ecosystem that inspired Minerva Hoyt to seek federal protection for what is now Joshua Tree National Park.

There are several century-old and 1920s-era gardens in this book. The justly famed and world-class gardens at the Huntington Library in San Marino were begun in 1904. Work on the Virginia Robinson Gardens in Beverly Hills started in 1912. Like all the gardens described in this book, these two gardens were added to

The arched patio behind Casa del Herrero in Montecito frames views of a formal garden with Moorish and European elements.

and subtracted from over the ensuing decades. Filoli, in Woodside, is another European-style formal garden, begun in 1917, with long vistas, allées, fountains, pools, brick walls, and hedges that create separate garden rooms. Casa del Herrero (1925) in Montecito is a prime example of a house and garden created in the Hispano-Moorish style, as is the Adamson House (1929) in Malibu. In the 1920s, the Olmsted Brothers firm helped create the romantic gardens at Rancho Los Alamitos on California's southern coast. All these exceptional gardens come with equally exceptional houses that you can visit as part of your garden tour.

The Depression and the WPA

In 1929, the economy crashed and the Great Depression took hold. Needless to say, it was not an age when great estates were established—at least, not any with gardens that we can visit today. FDR's Works Progress Administration (WPA) created jobs—and a couple of public gardens, too. Those included the Berkeley Rose Garden and the Morcom Amphitheater of Roses in Oakland. Both feature beautiful stonework and reflect the Arts and Crafts aesthetic that was popular in the Bay Area into the 1930s.

Postwar and Midcentury Modern Gardens

The size and style of California gardens changed after World War II, with one outstanding exception. Lotusland was an existing 1920s estate that became the home and private garden fantasy of the flamboyant opera singer Ganna Walska when she moved there in the 1940s. You may think the gardens at Lotusland are over-the-top—they are, gloriously so—but personally, I can't help but admire a woman who, at the end of her plant-collecting life, sold her jewels to buy a million-dollar cycad collection.

Ordinary mortals with cash—but not that kind of cash—scaled down their homes and gardens. It was the dawn of midcentury modern design and there is no better example than the Hortense Miller Garden in Laguna Beach, with its modernist, glass-walled house perched over a canyon, surrounded by a native plant garden.

The 1960s saw the creation of two urban public gardens in Oakland: the Kaiser Center Roof Garden and the terraced gardens at the Oakland Museum of California, an architectural icon of the Brutalist style. The small but exquisite Sherman Library and Gardens in Corona del Mar was begun in 1966 in a style that evokes a private botanical garden.

ART GARDENS

Many gardens contain works of art, but there are also some newer California gardens created by artists. I call these art gardens. In the early 1980s, the Japanese-American artist and designer Isamu Noguchi created a remarkable landscape-sculpture called California Scenario for a public plaza in Costa Mesa. You have to pass through an office lobby to reach this small and relatively unknown art garden that uses stone, plants, and water in sculptural ways to comment on California's different landscapes.

Artist Robert Irwin's Central Garden at the Getty Center in Los Angeles, completed in 1997, is full of color, movement, and dazzling horticultural details and effects. And at Cornerstone Sonoma, you'll find an outdoor gallery of nine small, intriguing, site-specific art gardens designed by a roster of artists and landscape architects. All these art gardens expand the boundaries of what a garden is and how people interact with it.

BOTANICAL GARDENS

The need to preserve the indigenous flora of California—and of every other place on Earth—is now of critical importance. California's many excellent botanical gardens not only display fascinating plants from California and around the world, they serve as safe havens for plants that are endangered or threatened in their native habitats. Some of them, like the San Diego Botanic Garden and the UC Botanical Garden at Berkeley, are rescue gardens that literally save the lives of plants that have been illegally transported or stolen. The wonderful but little-known Quarryhill Botanical Garden near Sonoma is unique in that every plant specimen there was grown from wild-collected seeds or cuttings obtained during plant expeditions throughout Asia.

More and more California botanical gardens have created demonstration or native plant gardens to show how the aboriginal plants, trees, and shrubs of the region can be used to create home gardens in California today. After all, these are the plants that adapted to California's climate and thrived for thousands of years on their own, without irrigation. The wildlife of the region still depends on them for food, shelter, and survival.

Several of the botanical gardens in this book are specifically devoted to California native plants; if at all possible, visit them in the spring when they are in flower. An easily accessed site is the Arthur L. Menzies Garden of California Native Plants within the San Francisco Botanical Garden in Golden Gate Park. The newest botanical garden, the Forrest Deaner Native Plant Botanic Garden, is dedicated to plants of the East Bay and San Francisco region. Regional Parks Botanic Garden in Tilden Park near Berkeley, a WPA project that opened in 1940, contains a collection of plants gathered from all four zones that make up the California Floristic Province. That is also the case at Rancho Santa Ana Botanic Garden in Claremont, one of the first botanic gardens in California to collect, preserve, and display plants from around the state. The Santa Barbara Botanic Garden is another place where you can expand your knowledge of California's rich and fascinating floristic heritage.

I have to add a few words here about the many botanical gardens and arboreta associated with the University of California at its various campuses. The University of California (UC) Botanical Garden at Berkeley, the UC Santa Cruz Arboretum, and the Mildred E. Mathias Botanical Garden at UCLA all began as research and teaching gardens. They still are, but the funding from the once-great University of California public education system that kept these gardens alive has been consistently cut back. As a result, UC gardens have had to do a lot of community outreach and restructuring to become more accessible to the public. They are rich botanical resources, and if you love plants you will love visiting them.

THE CALIFORNIA FLORISTIC PROVINCE

The California landscape that we see today and associate with palm trees, citrus groves, lush gardens, and verdant green lawns, all in the middle of the desert, is a complete fabrication. If you'd arrived in California with Luther Burbank in 1875, you would have seen a very different landscape: one that was still relatively unexploited (except for gold) and still had vast tracts of undeveloped or minimally developed land. This book, with the exception of Joshua Tree National Park, is about human-made gardens. They could not exist without humans tending to them. But I want to give you a bit of background information to help you understand California's natural landscape and the native plants found within it.

The United States has thirteen floristic provinces, each characterized by its own unique plant distributions based on climate, geology, and geography. Four of these thirteen biotic provinces occur within the state of California: Californian, Vancouverian,

Sonoran, and Great Basin. Together, these four bits of distinct botanical zones make up what is called the California Floristic Province. The nomenclature here is a bit confusing and you may be wondering what the difference between the California Floristic Province and the Californian floristic province is. Simply put, "California Floristic Province" refers to all four floristic provinces together (when conjoined, these four zones cover the entire state of California); the Californian floristic province is only one of the four provinces within the larger California Floristic Province.

Most of the gardens in this guide lie within the Californian floristic province, which is characterized by a Mediterranean climate—that is, cool, moist winters and hot, dry summers. The same climatic conditions are found in just four other places on Earth: Mediterranean Europe, South Africa, Chile, and a small part of Australia. Although it is the smallest of North America's floristic provinces, the Californian province has the greatest diversity of plants north of Mexico. The plants that grow naturally in this climate can survive long periods without water and have adapted strategies to regenerate after the wildfires that are a regular part of this ecosystem. Coastal sage scrub (buckwheats and sages), southern maritime chaparral (tough evergreen shrubs like manzanita and chamise), oak woodlands, and grasslands are all part of the Californian floristic province, and you will see remnants or examples of them all in the gardens featured in this book.

If you visit the Mendocino Coast Botanical Gardens on the North Coast, you'll be in the Vancouverian floristic province. It's essentially a southern extension of the temperate coastal rainforests of the Pacific Northwest. The climate is cooler and wetter, fostering the growth of mixed evergreen and coniferous forests. Pines, madrones, and California's iconic coast and Sierra redwoods are all found in the Vancouverian province.

Giant cacti and desert scrub characterize plant life in the Sonoran zone. Although you will encounter several stunning cacti gardens in this book, the actual Sonoran floristic province in California covers only the northwestern edge of this enormous desert system. You can experience it in Joshua Tree National Park near Palm Springs.

The Great Basin region of California's four-zone floristic province is high-elevation desert that lies east of the Cascade and Sierra Nevada mountain ranges. It is magnificent country, covered with sagebrush—but we won't be going there in this guide.

A quiet spot at Sunnylands Center and Gardens, one of California's newest public gardens, near Palm Springs.

HOW THIS GUIDE IS ORGANIZED

The fifty gardens I write about in this book span an area of roughly 685 miles, from Mendocino, on the northern coast, to San Diego, near the Mexican border. That's a lot of ground to cover, so I've divided the book into two parts, Northern California and Southern California. Within those two halves (some might think of them as separate states), I've further divided the book into geographic or urban regions. This will make it easier to plan your tours if you want to visit several gardens in the same vicinity. The maps will give you a quick overview and geographical summary of where the gardens are located.

Northern California Gardens

My Northern California chapter begins with San Francisco and the San Francisco Peninsula. Magnificent and multi-gardened Golden Gate Park dominates the City by the Bay, and a short, scenic ferry ride across that bay takes you to the surprisingly picturesque gardens at Alcatraz. The Peninsula, extending south from San Francisco, includes places like Palo Alto and Saratoga, where you'll find a historic estate, Montalvo, and the second-oldest Japanese garden in the United States, Hakone. Woodside is the home of Filoli, the greatest estate garden in Northern California.

The East Bay section of the guide includes Berkeley, with its world-class botanical garden; Oakland, with its iconic midcentury modern rooftop and museum gardens; and two botanic gardens devoted to California's native plants: the Forrest Deaner Native Plant Botanic Garden in historic Benicia and the Regional Parks Botanic Garden in Tilden Park near Berkeley. A true East Bay garden gem, the Ruth Bancroft Garden, is located in Walnut Creek.

Cross the Golden Gate Bridge to find the unique assortment of gardens featured in the Sonoma and Vicinity section. From the contemporary art gardens created at Cornerstone Sonoma to the historic grounds of the Marin Art and Garden Center and the wild-collected Asian specimen plants at Quarryhill Botanical Garden, you'll find plenty to whet your garden-loving appetite. You can also visit the home and experimental farm of Luther Burbank (who created so many new plant varieties that he became known as the "Wizard of Santa Rosa"), enjoy a glass of local wine, and stroll through a lovely garden at Ferrari-Carano Vineyards and Winery.

Three very different garden destinations are included in the Central and North Coast section. The much-loved Mendocino

Young and old enjoy exploring Robert Irwin's art garden at the Getty Center in Los Angeles.

Coast Botanical Gardens are the only botanical gardens in the continental United States with plantings right along the Pacific Ocean. Monterey, with its bevy of charming "secret" gardens arrayed around some of the oldest buildings in California, is another fabulous garden-themed destination. At the UC Santa Cruz Arboretum, you'll find the largest collection of Australian plants outside of Australia.

Southern California Gardens

Forget about those celluloid stars of the silver screen. The real stars in the Los Angeles and Vicinity section are the ones planted in the ground—A-list gardens that will amaze and delight house and garden lovers. Did you know you can visit the very first estate in Beverly Hills—and that it has one of California's most exquisite gardens? It's called the Virginia Robinson Gardens and it's unforgettable. If you want some good old-fashioned Hollywood scandal and extravagance to go with your garden touring, it's just a hop and skip from Virginia Robinson's place to Greystone Mansion and Gardens, built for a wealthy California oilman. Two gardens in Malibu more than make up for the crowded commute out to the beach. The Adamson House, built in the 1920s above the white sands of Surfrider Beach, is lavishly decorated with tiles made at Malibu Potteries. A short distance and 2,000 years away is the Getty Villa, a superlative re-creation of a Roman garden-villa that was buried under ash spewed out by Mt. Vesuvius in 79 A.D. The garden created by Robert Irwin at the Getty Center high above Los Angeles is a dazzling work of contemporary landscape art. Not far from it is the Mildred E. Mathias Botanical Garden at UCLA, stuffed with botanical treasures.

And speaking of treasures, if there's one California garden that almost every garden lover has heard about and dreams of making a pilgrimage to, it's the botanical garden at the Huntington Library. You'll find this amazing early twentieth-century collection of rare books, rare art, and rare plants in the Pasadena and Vicinity section, along with three other botanical gardens that lucky locals use like parks. Descanso Gardens and the Los Angeles County Arboretum and Botanic Garden were both created from the private estates of larger-than-life figures. Anyone interested in California's fast-disappearing native flora should make a point to visit Rancho Santa Ana, which contains plants from all four zones that make up the entire California Floristic Province.

The five gardens I feature in the South Coast section run the gamut in terms of style and content. The gardens hidden behind the walls of the Sherman Library in Corona del Mar are a garden connoisseur's delight. Rancho Los Alamitos, a fascinating estate with an impeccably maintained historic ranch house and period gardens, is a must-see. Completely different but no less fascinating is California Scenario, the contemporary landscape garden in Costa Mesa created by the renowned artist and designer Isamu Noguchi. If you're a fan of midcentury modern design, put the Hortense Miller Garden in Laguna Beach on your South Coast list; created by an artist, it's perched in a protected canyon above the Pacific and surrounded by a garden of mostly native plants. The South Coast Botanic Garden in Palos Verdes was among the first gardens in the world to be created atop a landfill, but you'd never know that as you're exploring its rose garden and appealing plant collections.

One of the great gardens of California, a true reserve-in-advance-and-don't-miss-your-chance attraction, is Lotusland, described in the Santa Barbara and Vicinity section. You'll be dazzled and delighted as a guide shows you around the extravagant gardens created by Ganna Walska at her estate in Montecito. Just minutes away is another marvel of Montecito, Casa del Herrero, with its historic house and gardens from the 1920s. Nearby, the Santa Barbara Botanic Garden showcases California native plants in a grand and historic landscape.

Are you interested in desert gardens? Have a look at the Palm Springs and Vicinity section. The new Sunnylands Center and Gardens, a part of the Annenberg estate in Rancho Mirage, is a low-water, desert-themed delight. And what better place than Joshua Tree National Park to explore a true, unwatered desert landscape where you can get up close and personal with cacti and succulents in their native habitat?

In San Diego and Vicinity, you'll find Balboa Park, one of California's greatest public spaces, which contains several fascinating gardens. And the San Diego Botanic Garden is home to a lush and colorful assortment of tropical and Mediterranean plants and a renowned collection of cycads, among the oldest plants on Earth.

As you can see, it's quite a diverse list and it provides a lot of exciting garden-touring possibilities. It's a selective list but it is thorough in terms of presenting the best and most interesting California gardens to visit. If a garden isn't worth at least a half-hour of your time, it's not included. Some, of course, need two hours or more for a leisurely exploration.

DROUGHT AND WATER ISSUES

California was in an extended period of drought as I visited all these gardens. And all the garden personnel, without exception, were well aware of that fact. Watering was a huge issue and will remain so into the future, whether this drought cycle abates or not. But the amazing thing was that even in the midst of the drought, the gardens were glorious.

Some, however, had plants that were experiencing periods of early bloom (three to four weeks earlier than usual) and premature leaf drop. Some water-loving trees (like redwoods) were showing signs of stress. When the state mandated a thirty percent reduction in the use of water, the gardens without private sources of water met and sometimes exceeded that goal. Watering was reduced, a few of the verdant lawns associated with great estate gardens were allowed to go brown, and many fountains were turned off. But all the cacti, succulents, and native plants—the ones adapted to long periods of low or no water—were doing just fine.

The fact is, California has always experienced periods of drought. Drought is part of a cyclical pattern in Mediterranean climates, but climate change has exacerbated the problem. Over the past decades, however, as more and more water has been "harvested" from the Colorado and every other river in the state, many Californians and visitors have grown accustomed to the idea that water in California is a resource that will never run dry. There's a whole lot of rethinking going on in the California garden world.

Here are a couple of tips to help you enjoy these wonderful gardens to the fullest. If at all possible, visit in the spring, from March through May, when native plants, wildflowers, and established garden plants have been revived by whatever winter rains have fallen. If you are garden touring later in the summer, lower your expectations a bit and don't expect Technicolor green lawns or every garden plant to look its best.

By the way, none of my photos in this book have been recolored or enhanced in any way. As you can see, drought does not eradicate the brilliant colors, forms, and textures you'll find in California gardens.

VISITING THE GARDENS

Every garden in this book is open to the public. If it's a park, like Golden Gate Park or Balboa Park, you can just walk in any time of the day. But many of the other gardens have opening and closing times, closed days, or reservation requirements. Before you go, check the website or call to make sure the garden is going to be open on the day you want to visit.

To get into the Virginia Robinson Gardens in Beverly Hills, Lotusland and Casa del Herrero in Montecito, and the Hortense Miller Garden in Laguna Beach, you must make a reservation in advance. Don't be put off by the need to do this—each of these gardens is worth the effort. This advance reservation system is necessary because these four special gardens were bequeathed to cities or counties by their owners; the neighbors, not wanting to see their streets turned into parking lots, have put restrictions on the number of visitors per day. You will get directions to the gardens when you make your reservation, and a docent-led tour when you arrive. No advance reservation is necessary at Filoli, also in the pantheon of great California gardens.

You can take a self-guided tour of the gardens at Rancho Los Alamitos, but if you want to visit the ranch house—I highly recommend you do—you must also make arrangements in advance. The same is true at the Luther Burbank Home and Gardens in Santa Rosa. The Getty Villa in Malibu and the Getty Center in Los Angeles are free, but you must reserve a parking space in advance (and pay for it) in order to get in.

If you're driving, it's possible in many cases to visit two or more gardens in one day, provided they are in the same geographic region or neighborhood. The maps will give you a better idea of what gardens are close to one another. A few quick suggestions: Sherman Library and Hortense Miller Garden; Lotusland and Casa del Herrero; Virginia Robinson Garden and Greystone Mansion and Gardens; Cornerstone Sonoma and Quarryhill Botanical Garden. You can easily reach Golden Gate Park, Balboa Park in San Diego, and some of the other gardens by public transportation. Most, however, require a car.

SUPPORT THE GARDENS

Most public gardens are not-for-profit organizations. To keep their gates open and their plants growing, they depend on membership and admission fees, grants, donors, plant sales, and gift

A brilliant bougainvillea blooms beside the eighteenth-century bell tower at the old Carmel Mission in Carmel-by-the-Sea.

shop sales. Volunteers are essential to their operation and ongoing maintenance. If there is a public garden in your vicinity, support it. Become a member, or join the garden's team of docents and volunteers. Help to keep these unique and valuable treasures open and available to all.

HAPPY GARDEN TOURING

The public gardens I've included in this book tell a tale of plant loving, plant collecting, and plant protecting, from the time of California's earliest native peoples right up to the present day. That's the wonderful thing about garden touring: not only are the gardens dazzling and inspiring places to visit, they provide a horticultural history lesson that ties you to a place and an era, introducing you to all kinds of fascinating personalities. I hope you will find this a useful, informative, and entertaining guide for your garden touring adventures in the Golden State.

Fort
Bragg

Mendocino Coast
Botanical Gardens

Coast
Ranges

1

Point
Arena

Pacific
Ocean

580 Richmond

Blake Garden

Regional Parks Botanic Garden
and Tilden Nature Area

Berkeley
Rose Garden

Angel
Island

San
Francisco
Bay

80 Berkeley

University of California
Botanical Garden at Berkeley

Sausalito

Morcom
Amphitheater
of Roses

Treasure
Island

101

Alcatraz

80

Oakland

Kaiser
Center
Roof
Garden

Golden
Gate

Presidio of
San Francisco

Oakland Museum
of California

San
Francisco

880

Golden Gate
Park

280

Alameda

San Francisco
Botanical Garden

northern

california

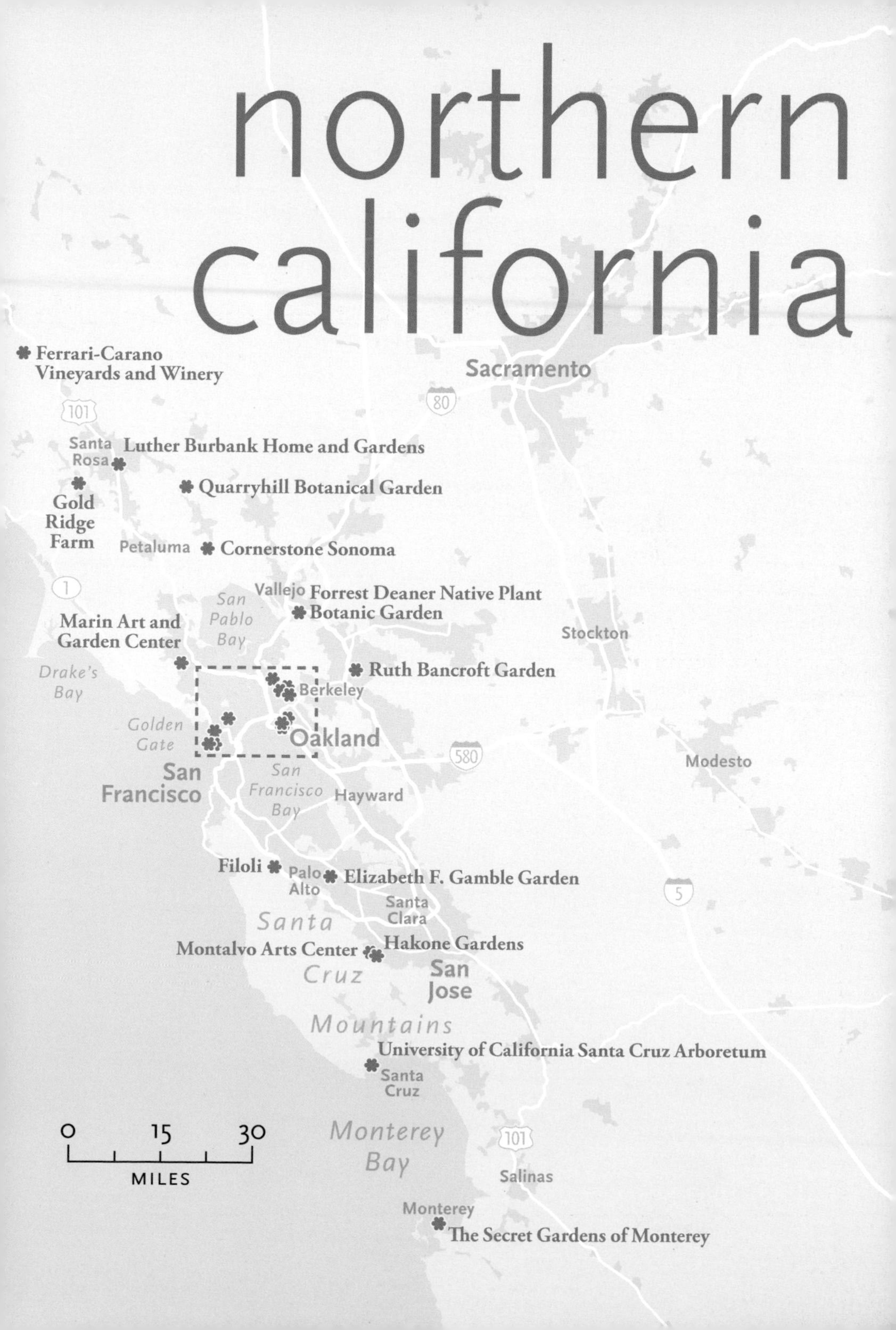

✿ Ferrari-Carano
Vineyards and Winery

Sacramento

101

Santa
Rosa ✿ Luther Burbank Home and Gardens

✿ Quarryhill Botanical Garden

✿ Gold
Ridge
Farm

Petaluma ✿ Cornerstone Sonoma

Vallejo ✿ Forrest Deaner Native Plant
        ✿ Botanic Garden

San
Pablo
Bay

Stockton

Marin Art and
Garden Center

Drake's
Bay

✿ Ruth Bancroft Garden

Berkeley

Golden
Gate

✿ Oakland

San
Francisco

San
Francisco
Bay

Hayward

Modesto

580

Filoli ✿ Palo ✿ Elizabeth F. Gamble Garden
        Alto

Santa
Clara

5

Santa
Cruz
Mountains

Montalvo Arts Center ✿ ✿ Hakone Gardens

San
Jose

University of California Santa Cruz Arboretum

✿ Santa
Cruz

Monterey
Bay

101

Salinas

Monterey

✿ The Secret Gardens of Monterey

One of the most famous spans in the world, the Golden Gate Bridge opened in 1937 and connects San Francisco to Marin County and the rest of Northern California.

san francisco
& peninsula

alcatraz

Alcatraz Island, San Francisco Bay, San Francisco, CA 94133
nps.gov/alca (National Park Service); alcatrazgardens.org
    (garden information)
Visit year-round; March–June offers best weather and
    maximum blooms

- 📞 (415) 561-4900 (National Park Service); (415) 981-7625
  (to purchase tickets)
- 🕐 Open daily year-round except Thanksgiving, Dec 25, and
  Jan 1; gardens accessible only via docent-led garden
  tours Fri and Sun at 9:45am; gardens at Officers' Row
  open to public on Wed 11am–2pm (ferries to the island
  leave from Pier 33 at Embarcadero and Bay Street in San
  Francisco about every half-hour starting at 9am; reserve
  ferry ticket well in advance)
- $ Garden admission free, admission fee for ferry to
  Alcatraz National Park
- ♿ Some portions of tour unsuitable for wheelchairs and
  those with limited mobility
- 🐕 No dogs

Surprisingly beautiful gardens grown by prisoners and staff in an unexpected setting

One of the most fascinating garden tours you'll ever take is on the notorious island of Alcatraz, or The Rock.

Gardens at Alcatraz? Yes, and beautiful gardens they are. So beautiful, in fact, that at times you might think you're strolling on a lush Mediterranean isle instead of the grounds of a maximum-security prison that once housed the likes of Al Capone, Bugsy Malone, and Baby Face Nelson. As an added bonus you'll enjoy spectacular views of San Francisco Bay, the San Francisco skyline, and Golden Gate Bridge.

You can see sections of the gardens without taking the docent-led tour, but if you're looking for a unique garden experience,

Lush gardens like the ones on West Road amaze most visitors to Alcatraz.

book a seat on one of the first two ferries on a Friday or Sunday and hook up with the 9:45am tour that leaves from the Alcatraz boat landing.

Alcatraz Island served as a federal penitentiary from 1933 to 1963. Only the most "incorrigible" criminals from other prisons were sent there. The island became a national park, part of the Golden Gate National Recreation Area, in 1972. But Alcatraz was not always a prison, and the island's story goes back to the earliest years of California statehood.

The Rock is just that: a 60- to 125-million-year-old chunk of solid greywacke sandstone sitting in the middle of San Francisco Bay, about 1.5 miles from shore. The tiered configuration you see today, with a switchback road leading up to the top, was blasted out of the rock in the 1850s. In 1854, the first lighthouse on the West Coast was erected on the island and, apparently, the first garden was planted—by the lighthouse keeper. The island became a military fortification during the Gold Rush and expanded during the Civil War, when houses were erected for officers and a citadel was built. By the 1880s, in part because of an island beautification

Colorful and picturesque, the gardens at Alcatraz were first planted over a hundred years ago when the island was an army fort.

program, gardens were planted along the road, on the terraces, around the officers' houses, and on the topmost citadel. But gardening is obviously impossible on solid rock, so precious soil had to be hauled over from the mainland.

The gardens on Alcatraz today were mostly planted during the island's thirty-year prison era. Two people in particular helped to create them. Fred Reichel, the warden's secretary, took it upon himself to maintain the Victorian-style flower gardens left behind by the army. Reichel also obtained plants that do well in Mediterranean climates and taught inmates how to build, plant, and maintain the gardens. One of those inmates was Elliott Michener, a counterfeiter who'd been moved from Leavenworth. Michener spent eight years helping to build gardens on the west side of the island—part of another attempt to make The Rock look more appealing from San Francisco—and was eventually promoted to gardener of the Warden's House. The experience of gardening literally transformed Michener's life, giving him, as he later said, "a lasting interest in creativity."

When Alcatraz was decommissioned as a federal penitentiary in 1963, the gardens were abandoned. Most of the flowers disappeared, but some of the Mediterranean plants that Reichel had obtained and men like Michener had planted were so tough that they are still blooming today. They're called, appropriately enough, "survivor plants." About 230 of the approximately 600 plant species on Alcatraz are survivors. The Park Conservancy has consulted historic photographs and documentation to restore the gardens but it also uses sustainable drought-resistant plants to approximate some of the original plant stock.

You'll see remnants of the earliest military-era gardens and your first survivor plants—an Australian tea tree (*Melaleuca alternifolia*) and a giant Mexican yucca—as you leave the ferry landing and head up toward the Sally Port, the restored entrance to the nineteenth-century fort. Beyond it, a verdant rock wall covered with ferns, mature ivy, wild plum, and an eighty-year-old pinkish white fuchsia stretches along the main road.

At the end of the wall, most visitors turn and continue up the slope toward the cellblock. If you're on the garden tour, however, you continue straight on and get to enter the lovely Rose Garden. This garden was once filled with roses planted by army families during the island's military era, and cared for by Fred Reichel after they left. In 1989, the Heritage Rose Group found, took cuttings of, and replanted about fifteen rose species that had survived nearly three decades of complete neglect. One survivor was the beautiful pinkish red *Rosa* 'Bardou Job', which originated in Wales but could no longer be found in its native land. You can see this old Welsh beauty growing on the terrace balustrade overlooking the bay (cuttings have also been returned to Wales). In addition to fragrant old roses, the Rose Garden is planted with colorful spring bulbs and an array of bright perennials; a new greenhouse stands on the site of the old one. The towering rock wall that rises behind this flower-filled terrace always reminds me of a medieval European castle.

One level up, Officers' Row is another garden area that you can enter only if you're on the garden tour. These sheltered gardens, filled with brilliant red pelargoniums, white calla lilies, and springtime iris, were created on the foundations of three large Victorian houses torn down in 1941.

Near the top, just below the entrance to the grim cellblock (the main destination for most visitors), you'll come to the empty shell of the Warden's House. The lush, succulent-filled plot beside it was the garden personally cared for by Elliott Michener, the counterfeiter turned gardener, shortly before he was paroled. This area overlooks the Parade Ground down at shore level. During spring nesting season, the Parade Ground is closed off to protect the western gulls, snowy egrets, brants, cormorants, and oystercatchers that make their home on the island.

The West Road takes you along the west side of the island, passing through gardens that are open to all visitors. What makes this side of the island so remarkable is the lush assortment of succulents planted along the exposed slopes. Here you'll see the big, bold *Agave attenuata*—sometimes called foxtail or swan's neck agave because of its long, curving stalks—and a host of multihued sedums that create an eye-popping display.

The terraces below the small wooden tool shed used by Elliott Michener and his inmate work crew are planted with rambling roses; survivor fuchsias; apple, pear, and fig trees; and masses of *Echium candicans* (pride of Madeira), with its stiff, dramatic, purple-blue flower stalks.

The empty shell of the Warden's House at Alcatraz overlooks gardens planted in Officers' Row by prison employees and inmates.

For me, the gardens at Alcatraz have a resonance that goes way beyond their obvious beauty. A century of gardening by employees and inmates has left a rich and moving testament to the human need to connect with nature and create beauty under even the harshest of conditions. It's not easy to turn a rock into a garden—but they did it.

filoli

86 Canada Road, Woodside, CA 94062
filoli.org
Visit mid-April and May for maximum
    blooms

📞 (650) 364-8300
🕐 Open early Feb–Oct Tues–Sat
    10am–3:30pm, Sun 11am–3:30pm;
    closed Nov–early Feb and major
    holidays
$ Admission fee
♿ Some lawn areas and narrow
    pathways are unsuitable for
    wheelchairs or strollers

🐕 No dogs

A gilded, spectacular garden dream of a bygone era

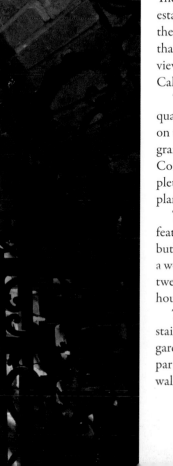

Inviting portals lead visitors into the magnificent Filoli gardens.

William Bowers Bourn had a credo: "To fight for a just cause; to love your fellow man; to live a good life." Take the first two letters of "fight," "love," and "live" and what do you have? Filoli, the extraordinary garden estate Bourn built about thirty miles south of San Francisco. With its Gilded Age house and Golden Age garden, Filoli is a glamorous memory of lives lived on a grand scale in a setting of incomparable beauty. It has no peer in Northern California and is now a National Historic Landmark.

Filoli was built on the gold that came from gold—namely, the Empire Gold Mine in Grass Valley. The owner of the mine, William Bowers Bourn II, bought 654 acres in the foothills of the Santa Cruz Mountains at the south end of Crystal Springs Lake. The landscape supposedly reminded him of Muckross, the Irish estate he'd purchased for his daughter Maud in 1910. Today, all the property surrounding Filoli is a protected watershed. What that means is that Filoli still enjoys the same valley and mountain views that it had over a century ago, a rarity in overdeveloped California.

The Bourns were San Franciscans, but after the 1906 earthquake, they, like many other wealthy families, built country estates on the Peninsula. Stylistically, everything that was considered grand, elegant, and "classy" back then originated on the East Coast or in Europe. That's why the palatial house at Filoli, completed in 1917, was built of bricks instead of wood and resembles a plantation in Virginia or a grand manor in England or Ireland.

The house has been beautifully preserved and has the kind of features we would expect in a mansion of that era: an enormous butler's pantry, walk-in safes converted into Western-themed bars, a wood-paneled library, and a dining room with a table that seats twenty. The dazzling floral arrangements seen throughout the house come from Filoli's own Cutting Garden.

The Bourns asked Bruce Porter, a San Francisco artist and stained-glass maker, to help design the sixteen acres of formal gardens. Porter's design, with lawns, terraces, parterres, and compartmented garden rooms framed by hedges, Irish yews, and brick walls, takes its cue from Renaissance-era European gardens. He was aided by Isabella Worn, a self-taught and highly regarded horticulturist from one of San Francisco's oldest families.

It's a thirsty garden, full of tender, water-loving, non-drought-resistant plants, but it was created at a time (between 1917 and 1921) when water was never an issue—especially since Bourn owned the Crystal Springs Reservoir at the end of the valley. The California drought and water restrictions have forced Filoli to let some lawns go brown and reduce watering, but if you visit from February through April, after the winter rains, you'll find the landscape lush and green.

The gardens achieved national renown when the estate was sold in 1937 to Mr. and Mrs. William Roth, owners of the Matson Navigation Company (their passenger steamships made the run from San Francisco to Hawaii). Mrs. Roth retained Isabella Worn as her chief gardener and together they brought the maturing gardens to a new level of perfection. Attention to detail is crucial in this kind of collector's garden and Filoli's eight full-time gardeners are up to the task.

There are many ways to explore the gardens at Filoli and there are many gardens to explore. As you approach the visitor center, you'll pass the olive orchard with its old Mission and Manzanillo olive trees. The entry courtyard of the house is embellished with a collection of mature magnolias, Japanese maples, Atlas cedars, and a grove of centuries-old coast live oaks, the native tree of the region. More exotic trees, including a sculpted New Zealand tea tree (*Leptospermum scoparium* 'Nichollsii Nanum'), a Chilean myrtle (*Luma apiculata*), and Hinoki cypresses (*Chamaecyparis obtusa*), are found on or near the upper terraces behind the house. In April, massive white and purple wisterias burst into fragrant flower along the terraces' carved stone balustrade and elsewhere in the garden.

Steps lead down into the romantic Sunken Garden, with its rectangular reflecting pool and side beds filled with the colorful seasonal displays Filoli is known for: tulips, daffodils, and other bulbs in the spring, tender annuals like petunias, zinnias, phlox, and impatiens in the summer. A beautiful brick wall with an intricately carved wooden gate (once the front door of the Bourn house in San Francisco) separates the Sunken Garden from Filoli's garden shop.

West of the Sunken Garden, a lush green lawn flanked by pollarded London plane trees leads to the brilliantly blue swimming

Spring plantings enliven the area around the reflecting pool at Filoli.

pool, installed by the Roths in the 1950s, and the pool pavilion, with landscaping by Isabella Worn. Have a look at the 1920s-era changing rooms to one side of the pool (used by tennis players before the pool was built). In front of the building there are two giant Camperdown elms (*Ulmus glabra* 'Camperdownii'), a non-reproducing cultivar created by grafting a Camperdown elm onto a Scotch elm.

Pass through the lovely garden house or one of three arched entrances to reach the Walled Garden. The garden house is an airy architectural confection that epitomizes the Belle Époque style of the early twentieth century. Gaston Rognier cast the six faces on the building's cornices and the two cast fruit baskets beside the stairway that leads down to a sundial with the inscription "Time began in a garden."

The Chartres Garden on the east side of the Walled Garden is an intricate design of boxwood parterres planted with blue and red annuals that are meant to resemble the luminous stained-glass windows at Chartres Cathedral. Within the Walled Garden you'll also find several rare specimens of pink-flowering mountain camellia (*Camellia reticulata*), a ginkgo (*Ginkgo biloba*) from southeast China, and a black beech (*Fuscospora solandri*) from New Zealand. A collection of blue and white hydrangeas is enclosed within a latticework fence.

More color-drenched gardens occupy the property south of the Walled Garden. First comes the Rose Garden, with over 500 roses, then the Elizabethan-style Knot Garden, created with germanders and lavender. Two raised display boxes are planted with herbs to re-create in miniature the designs of the Knot Garden. Running along the east side of these two gardens is a border of California perennials and a showy collection of tree peonies. In the center of this garden, the monumental yew allée (planted with about 200 dark Irish yews) marches across the lawn to the High Place at the southernmost end of the garden. From there, you can look down and see the layout of the entire garden, all its original views intact and framed within the green of the surrounding countryside. It's quite a sight.

West of the allée there's a wonderful fruit orchard, with over 1,200 fruit trees planted in 1918 to provide the Bourns with a year-round selection of dessert fruits. There's so much fruit grown here that Filoli holds a popular Autumn Festival at the end of September. Visitors can taste heritage apple varieties and other fruits grown and harvested at Filoli. The daffodil meadow in front of the orchard is at its peak in early March.

Just to the north, an entry gate in a brick wall opens into the secretive Woodland Garden. Here, in the deep shade, you'll find a host of camellias, Japanese maples, and other shade-loving plants.

As if all that weren't enough, you can also go hiking on five miles of nature trails among native redwoods and oaks. Almost everyone who visits Filoli comes away rapturous and determined to return. It's a kind of gilded, golden dream so uniquely of its time and place that it could never be replicated today.

This tranquil pool is an eye-catching feature in the long axis that runs the length of the gardens at Filoli.

elizabeth f. gamble garden

1431 Waverley Street, Palo Alto, CA 94301
gamblegarden.org
Visit early to late spring for overall color and bloom

- 📞 (650) 329-1356
- 🕐 Gardens open daily dawn to dusk; house open Mon–Fri 9am–2pm
- $ Admission free
- 🐕 No dogs

Early twentieth-century garden and house of an iconic American family

Elizabeth Gamble lived her entire life in the house her father built in 1902.

If you want to see what life was like in an earlier, sweeter, less complicated time, hitch up your buggy and head down to the Elizabeth Gamble house and garden in Palo Alto, about thirty-three miles south of San Francisco. When this house was built in 1902, Palo Alto—now the center of Silicon Valley—was a sleepy hamlet with dirt roads and no telephones. People got around by horse and carriage. If you had money—as the Gambles did—you could live a pretty golden life in rural Palo Alto.

You've heard of Procter & Gamble? That's the Gamble family we're talking about here. The son of the cofounder of P&G moved his wife, three sons, and daughter from Bourbon County, Kentucky, to Palo Alto, California, in 1901. The daughter was Miss Elizabeth Gamble; she remained Miss Elizabeth Gamble her entire life. After her parents died, she continued to live in the house with one of her brothers, George, until her death in 1981. If Tennessee Williams had gotten his hands on this scenario, he would no doubt have turned it into a gothic melodrama of lost dreams and unrequited love. And who knows, maybe that was part of Miss Elizabeth Gamble's life story. But taking care of her

garden was another part, as was her local charity work. She was very generous with her garden—now officially called the Elizabeth F. Gamble Garden Center—and opened it up to community groups for social events.

Like her three brothers, Elizabeth attended Stanford University. Unlike her brothers, she lasted only a year before deciding she wanted to study at Wellesley instead. After that, she traveled in Europe with one of her Irish aunts, even meeting the King of Prussia, before returning home to Palo Alto. She and George lived together for decades in the 5,000-square-foot Colonial Revival house their father had built in 1902.

It's difficult to know how much of the garden was Elizabeth's creation and how much is a legacy from the original garden design by Alan Reid. Over the years, Miss Gamble maintained the garden she had grown up in and dealt with all the vagaries, surprises, and calamities that gardeners have to contend with from year to year. She bequeathed her house and garden to the city of Palo Alto for public use. The city dithered for years over what to do with this historic property. Finally, they allowed the Garden Club of Palo Alto to purchase it for use as a community resource and public park, just as Miss Gamble would have wanted. The garden has had to adapt and change with the times and, luckily, the alterations have enriched the garden's mission to serve the public in a variety of ways.

Try to visit during the week, when the house is open, so you can get a more complete picture of what life was like inside and outside the Gamble house. It's a lovely, old-fashioned Edwardian ensemble, with the big, sturdy house set back from a circular drive once used for carriages. The front lawn is graced by two *Magnolia*

The vine-covered gazebo at the Elizabeth F. Gamble Garden is part of several newer gardens created behind the Edwardian-era house.

grandiflora trees and a towering Canary Island date palm. The gardens, on both sides and behind the house, cover about 2.5 acres.

Green lattice fencing and a mixed shrubbery border of different heights and textures serves to delineate space and create different garden rooms in the formal style typical of the era. Unfortunately, the once-beautiful weeping cherry trees that formed a locally famous allée to the right of the house fell victim to age and drought; the water-loving cherries have been replaced by crabapple trees that will eventually make quite a spring display. Fragrant olive trees and vivid pink crape myrtles are planted nearby. The allée looks down toward a grotto.

No garden of this period would have been considered complete without a rose garden. Gamble's circular rose garden has a romantic outer ring of white roses (*Rosa* 'Iceberg') underplanted with catmint (*Nepeta* ×*faassenii*) featuring lavender-blue flowers. Both heritage and modern roses occupy the center of the ring.

Another lovely period piece is the Wisteria Garden with original plantings of double lavender Japanese wisteria (*Wisteria floribunda* 'Violacea Plena') around the library's porch and the single-flowering straight species draping its spring-blooming flower clusters near a small fountain. Just beyond is the midcentury modern Tea House, a simple, attractive structure that Miss Gamble had built in 1948 as a venue for garden and community events. The neighboring Carriage House has also been adapted for use as a lecture room and a setting for public events. The impressive coast live oak (*Quercus agrifolia*) was here a century before the Gambles arrived.

Demonstration beds to the left of the house feature several newer garden beds that surround a modern but decidedly Victorian-looking gazebo used for vertical plantings of sweet autumn clematis (*Clematis terniflora*) and porcelain berry (*Ampelopsis brevipedunculata*). The demonstration beds include a Shade and Sun Garden, with salvias, mixed perennials, and trees; a Mediterranean Garden, with drought-tolerant euphorbias and mulleins; and a border, with tall ornamental grasses. Though it's not formal, heritage, or even eye-catching, one of my favorite demonstration plantings is called Roots & Shoots. This plot is tended entirely by third graders who get a rare hands-on opportunity to garden and watch things grow. It's an important introduction to nature that I wish every child could have in this day of endless screen-gazing, and I suspect Miss Elizabeth Gamble would agree.

golden gate park

What Central Park is to New York—
only larger and on the ocean

Bounded by Fulton Street, Lincoln Way, Stanyan Street, and the Pacific Ocean, San Francisco, CA 94118
goldengatepark.com
Visit year-round; February–June for maximum blooms

- 📞 (415) 831-2700
- 🕐 Park open daily year-round; Conservatory of Flowers daily 9:30am–5pm (Sun from 11am), closed Thanksgiving, Dec 25
- $ Admission free; fee for Conservatory of Flowers and de Young Museum
- 🚌 Public Transportation
- 🐕 Dogs on leash

The observation tower in the de Young Museum provides a bird's-eye view of the Music Concourse in Golden Gate Park.

Golden Gate Park can be counted among the great parks of the world. Give yourself as much time as you can to explore it, because there are surprises at every turn: exotic plants, two major museums, a national AIDS memorial, an ocean beach, windmills, lakes, a Victorian glasshouse, even a herd of bison. The San Francisco Botanical Garden is also located in Golden Gate Park, but I've given that a separate entry.

The Gold Rush of the 1850s brought tens of thousands of people and enormous wealth to San Francisco. The city fathers wanted a city park to show off the golden prosperity of their new metropolis—and to spur its continued development. In 1870, after eighteen years of negotiations, civic leaders finally gained control from the U.S. government of 1,017 acres of what was then called the "Outer Lands," and hired a surveyor to do an initial topographical study. There was just one problem: the proposed park site was nothing but thin sandy soil and sand dunes raked by ocean winds. When asked for his opinion, Frederick Law Olmsted, the designer of Central Park, dismissed the site as impossible.

William Hammond Hall was only twenty-five when he was awarded the surveyor's job (he'd submitted the lowest bid). Hall was a civil engineer with no knowledge of horticulture or landscape design. He learned fast and on his feet, and was hired to be the first superintendent of Golden Gate Park. Central Park in New York was the only other park of this size and scope in the country at that time and Hall, taking his cue from Olmsted (via Capability Brown), adopted the Picturesque style of landscaping with winding roads, walking paths, and natural features. In an age that didn't understand the concept of ecology, Hall had an intuitive sense of microclimates and the importance of native vegetation. No one was allowed to uproot any of the scrub oaks, scrub lupine, or wild willows that grew in the sandy soil of the park and around its eight (now five) lakes.

In 1871, Hall planted the first trees in the northeastern Panhandle section of the park: Monterey pines, Monterey cypresses, and about ten species of fast-growing eucalyptus. Some of these original trees can still be seen, though most are now gone. The coast live oaks in the Panhandle are some of the oldest trees in the city and a rare remnant of native vegetation.

Hall also began the process of reclaiming the sand dunes. He started by creating two drives that separated the beach from the park. But his work came to an abrupt end when a vindictive politician brought some trumped-up charges against him and he was forced to resign. For the next ten years all work in the park ceased. When a repentant board of supervisors asked Hall to return to his former post, he declined but recommended John McLaren for the job. It was an inspired choice. John McLaren took over as superintendent of Golden Gate Park in 1887 and remained in that position for fifty-three years. McLaren Lodge (55 Music Concourse Drive), the Moorish-Gothic building he lived in from 1890 until 1943, is still used as park headquarters.

A stern and demanding Scotsman, McLaren apprenticed as a landscape gardener on Scottish estates before emigrating to San Francisco. There, he created parks and gardens for nouveau riche Gold Rushers with new estates on the Peninsula. McLaren was a man who knew his plants and had very definite ideas about where to place them. Upward of 60,000 acacia trees were set out in one year; eventually, over half a million acacia trees of sixty different species were planted, along with more Monterey pines and cypresses. McLaren loved rhododendrons and planted hundreds of them in Hall's scenic rhododendron garden, now officially called the John McLaren Rhododendron Dell. Unlike Hall's naturalistic approach, McLaren favored the Mixed style of landscaping. Many of his gardens were symmetrical and strictly ornamental. The trees were planted for their utilitarian value as windbreaks as much as for their visual appeal.

That this autocratic yet self-effacing Scotsman had the park's best interests at heart was made clear when he was asked what he wanted as a birthday present and replied, "A hundred thousand tons of barnyard manure." He got his wish and used the manure as topsoil so he could finish planting the sand dunes—ecologically

The Conservatory of Flowers in Golden Gate Park survived the 1906 earthquake.

incorrect today, but a major feat back then. Horticultural historians might also be interested to note that McLaren was the one who introduced European beachgrass (*Ammophila arenaria*) as a way to bind the blowing sand of the dunes. He imported the grass seed from Vilmorin-Andrieux & Co., a seed company in Paris that dates back to 1743.

In 1879, after Hall's departure and before McLaren's arrival, the Conservatory of Flowers (100 John F. Kennedy Drive), one of the park's most famous buildings, was erected in the eastern

end of the park. This 12,000-square-foot Victorian glasshouse is the oldest building in the park and one of few such buildings in America. It was part of a prefabricated kit shipped to California to be erected on the Santa Clara estate of millionaire James Lick, but he died before it had been uncrated. A group of San Francisco's richest businessmen purchased the unassembled building and presented it to the city. Located in the Conservatory Valley area of the park, flanked on the east by the drought-tolerant Arizona Garden and on the west by the summer show-off Dahlia Garden, the ornate wood-and-glass conservatory with its central dome is home to some 1,700 species of aquatic and tropical plants, including orchids, giant waterlilies, and carnivorous plants. Beneficial insects and a crew of free-roaming geckos help keep insect pests at bay. The conservatory survived the 1906 earthquake, but many of the lawns, plants, and trees around it did not. They were destroyed by the huge number of homeless San Franciscans who poured into Conservatory Valley and camped out in a giant tent city erected by the military.

The National AIDS Memorial Grove (aidsmemorial.org) at the intersection of Bowling Green and Middle Drive is a beautiful living tribute to those who have died from AIDS and those who

Tranquil Stow Lake is one of five lakes found in Golden Gate Park.

have shared the victims' love and struggles. San Francisco was devastated by the AIDS epidemic and the lack of a national response to it. The memorial was proposed in 1988 as a place of remembrance and healing; in 1991 a team of landscape architects, gardeners, and volunteers began the work of reclaiming the seven-acre de Laveaga Dell. Today this area, privately funded and maintained by volunteers, is both tranquil and deeply moving. From the Circle of Friends plaza with its inscribed pavement, pathways lead down to a grassy meadow with a bank of perennial flowers and into a woodland area with redwoods, dogwoods, oaks, and pines. The shaded woodland, dotted with inscribed Sierra rock memorials, leads to the Fern Grotto, with towering tree ferns. In 1996, primarily because of the efforts of U.S. Congresswoman Nancy Pelosi, Congress designated this area a national memorial, the first of its kind in the United States.

West of here, you'll come to a sunken open-air plaza called the Music Concourse. This area, with its French park–style grid of pollarded London plane trees and wych elms, was created to attract visitors to the Midwinter International Exposition of 1894 (the country was one year into a major economic depression and it was hoped the exhibition would stir up business). The focal point of the basin was the Spreckels Temple of Music, better known as the Bandshell, where concerts are still given on Sunday afternoons.

The recently revitalized Music Concourse is surrounded by a host of major attractions and is a busy place. On the north side is the de Young Museum (deyoung.famsf.org), which opened in 2005, replacing an earlier building erected for the 1894 exhibition. Even if you don't want to look at the collections of modern art, step inside this copper-clad building (that is gradually acquiring a natural green patina) to have a look at the interior courtyard gardens. Then take the elevator to the top of the tower to enjoy a free and fabulous bird's-eye view of the park and the city.

Another new and noteworthy building, this one on the south side of the Music Concourse, is the Academy of Sciences (calacademy.org), a state-of-the-art natural history museum that replaces an earlier science museum erected in 1924. The country's only LEED-platinum museum building, the Academy of Sciences features a 2.5-acre living garden roof planted with California native plants.

The five-acre Japanese Tea Garden, located just west of the Music Concourse, is the oldest Japanese garden in the United States. It was originally part of a Japanese Village exhibit built for the 1894 exhibition. The garden was built by George Turner Marsh, an Australian businessman who had lived in Japan and was fascinated by Japanese culture. At the time, Asian cultures were considered exotic and most people had never seen such a garden. When the exhibition ended, the city decided to retain the charming tea garden that had been such a success with visitors. A Japanese landscape designer, Makoto Hagiwara, became the caretaker and guardian of the garden, living there with his family until his death in 1925. His family continued to maintain the garden until 1942 when they, along with all Japanese-Americans in the United States, were interned in concentration camps for the duration of World War II. Their residence was demolished and their personal collection of dwarf pines was removed and sold (they were returned to the park in 1965). Several original architectural features remain in this serene little gem of a garden, featuring carefully pruned Japanese maples, stands of bamboo, an old wisteria, koi ponds, and blossoming cherry trees in the spring.

Andy Goldsworthy's *Spire* in the Presidio was created in 2008 from fallen eucalyptus trees.

On the shores of Stow Lake, to the west, you can visit the Chinese Pavilion and climb Strawberry Hill with its waterfall and rustic stone bridges. Much of the park between Stow Lake and the ocean is given over to recreational pursuits. Closer to the park's western edge, you'll find the bison paddock, with its small herd of American bison. This iconic mammal had been hunted almost to extinction by 1891, when the first bison were brought to the park. The paddock was created in 1899 in an effort to breed the animals in captivity. The older bison you see today are descendants of a herd purchased in 1984 by Mayor Diane Feinstein's husband. Additional animals were acquired in 2011.

Two recently restored historic windmills stand at the western edge of the park. The North (Dutch) Windmill was erected in 1903 and used to draw fresh water for use in the park. The Queen Wilhelmina Tulip Garden beside it is ablaze with tulips in the spring. The South (Murphy) Windmill was once considered to be the largest Dutch-style windmill in the world. Both structures have undergone repairs and renovation in recent years.

And then—you can't go any farther because you've reached the Pacific Ocean. You might want to check out the Spanish Revival–style Beach Chalet, built in 1925 for use as a bathing facility and lounge. Like so much in Golden Gate Park, it has lived through decades of use, reuse, misuse, disuse, and rediscovery. The murals inside, showing scenes of everyday life in San Francisco, were painted in 1936–37 as a WPA project by the French-born artist and designer Lucien Labaudt. One of the figures depicted is John McLaren. The only other memorial to this hardworking and conscientious keeper and planter of Golden Gate Park is a bronze statue in the Rhododendron Dell. The dour McLaren hated statues and eschewed public adulation. He hid the statue of himself in his house and it wasn't placed in the park, amid the rhododendrons he loved, until after his death in 1943 at age ninety-six.

Presidio of San Francisco

In 1994, the Presidio of San Francisco, at the northern end of the Peninsula, became part of the Golden Gate National Recreation Area. This former military base, claimed by the Spanish in 1776 and taken by the United States in 1846 after twenty years of Mexican rule, offers trails, beaches, historic structures, and fabulous views of the Golden Gate Bridge. If you're driving to Golden Gate Park, consider including the Presidio in your visit. Start at San Francisco's oldest building, the Presidio Officers' Club (50 Morago Avenue; presidio.gov; open Tues–Sun 10am–6pm; admission free), now a cultural and visitor center. An Andy Goldsworthy nature-related ephemeral artwork, *Earth Wall*, is disintegrating right outside. Not far away is another Goldsworthy piece, *Spire*, made from some of the century-old eucalyptus trees that are now being removed from the Presidio. Goldsworthy laid stripped eucalyptus trunks end to end to create a third piece, *Wood Line*. If you're a movie buff, you'll probably want to visit Fort Point, where Kim Novak jumped into the Bay in Hitchcock's *Vertigo*.

hakone gardens

21000 Big Basin Way, Saratoga, CA 95070
hakone.com
Visit year-round; February for camellias, April for wisteria

- 📞 (408) 741-4994
- 🕐 Open Mon–Fri 10am–4pm (Mar–Nov until 5pm), Sat–Sun 11am–5pm; closed Dec 25, Jan 1
- $ Admission fee
- ♿ Raked gravel paths and stairways make parts of the garden unsuitable for wheelchairs and those with limited mobility
- 🐕 No dogs

The second-oldest Japanese-style garden in the country, with significant cultural and historical significance

Hakone Gardens is a rare treasure in more ways than one. The fact that this historic Japanese garden, among the oldest in the Western Hemisphere, survives at all is a testament to a collective garden-loving spirit that has kept it alive and growing for a hundred years. The garden has gone through many hands and modes of support and maintenance in that time. Recently, the National Trust for Historic Preservation selected Hakone Gardens as one of twelve sites in the country to receive their Save America's Treasures award.

Nestled in the hills of Saratoga, about fifty miles south of San Francisco, Hakone Gardens is just minutes away from Montalvo Arts Center with its Italianate villa and gardens. You can easily visit both on the same day—in fact, I'd encourage you to do so, because the two places were built about the same time and represent two entirely different garden and landscape philosophies.

Hakone's story begins in 1915 at the Pan-Pacific Exposition in San Francisco. Isabel Stine, a wealthy patron of the arts, was so enthralled by the Japanese pavilion and garden that she decided

A gentle spring rain adds to the timeless beauty of Hakone Gardens.

56 northern california

to create a similar place as a country retreat on the eighteen acres she and her husband Oliver had purchased in Saratoga. Isabel was nothing if not thorough: she sailed to Japan and spent a year looking at various garden estates, especially those in Hakone National Park, and hired a Japanese architect, Tsunematsu Shintani, and landscape designer, Naoharu Aihara, to help realize her plans. Given the rising tide of anti-Japanese sentiment in California at the time (Senator James Phelan, who built nearby Montalvo, worked to ban Japanese immigration entirely), Stine's hiring of Shintani and Aihara was a gesture of cross-cultural goodwill, a mission still carried on by the Hakone Foundation.

In 1917, Aihara set about creating a hill-and-pond garden, a style popular in seventeenth-century Japan and well suited for the Stines' hillside property. Like all Japanese gardens, the hill-and-pond style is meant for gentle strolling and viewing of the garden landscape in every season and from many different viewpoints. Shintani designed the wooden Moon Viewing House that sits on the hillside with a veranda overlooking the garden. This ensemble of house above and garden below is the original composition from 1917. The Stines did not live in the Moon Viewing House but in the three-bedroom Lower House, built in 1922 and now used as an events space.

Opera buffs take note: the West Coast premiere of Puccini's *Madama Butterfly* took place at Hakone Gardens under the sponsorship of Isabel Stine, who sat on the board of the San Francisco Opera. This was not a full-fledged production with orchestra, but introduced the work to an invited audience. Several decades later, Hakone Gardens was used as a setting in the 2005 movie *Memoirs of a Geisha*.

In 1932 the estate was sold to Major C. L. Tilden (Tilden Park in Berkeley is named for him; he helped to preserve land for public use throughout the Bay Area). The major put in the impressive main gate, and it was probably because he owned the place that Hakone Gardens made it through World War II, a time when Japanese-Americans were incarcerated in camps and many Japanese gardens were destroyed. The garden passed on to Tilden's sister. Her son put Hakone up for sale in 1961, and the estate was sold to six couples (four of them Japanese-Americans), who maintained the gardens and used Hakone as a kind of joint-custody time-share. After five years, that partnership sold the property to the city of Saratoga for use as a county park. A Kyoto-trained landscape architect was hired to begin restoration efforts. Eventually the Hakone Foundation was formed to take over maintenance and turn the park into an Asian-American cultural center.

Inevitably, over time and with the introduction of building and safety codes, Hakone Gardens has seen changes, additions, and modifications to the original design. The traditional earthen bridge, for instance, was closed to foot traffic and planted with 200 camellias. The Lower Wisteria Pavilion was built next to the pond and the Wisteria Arbor was added to one side of the house. The Tea Garden and Zen Garden were installed. In 1987 Kiyoshi Yasui, a fourteenth-generation architect to the Japanese imperial

Rare tortoiseshell bamboo was planted in the Bamboo Garden at Hakone Gardens.

family, was brought over to oversee the installation of the Bamboo Garden and Cultural Exchange Center. The design, construction, and restoration of the gardens has been facilitated by Ogata Kai, a group of landscape architects from Japan.

Once you've entered the main gate, start your tour with the classic view of the Moon Viewing House and Hill and Pond Garden seen from the Wisteria Pavilion. The irregularly shaped pond with its short, arched moon bridge is a traditional element in Japanese gardens, as is the tortoise-shaped island, a symbol of longevity. Tightly pruned shrubs and a tall Hinoki cypress (a tree often used in bonsai) add to the sculptured look of the scene while a small waterfall adds movement. Three stone lanterns and large carved and natural rocks are carefully sited around the pond as additional focal points.

There are various ways to explore the gardens from here. A pathway leads up past the waterfall and a bed of azaleas to the Moon Viewing House, where you can contemplate the same garden scene from above. Stairs to the left of the pavilion take you to the Bamboo Garden. This hillside garden is planted with several varieties of bamboo, including the rare and beautifully colored tortoiseshell bamboo from Japan. A winding path leads from the Bamboo Garden to the Moon Viewing House with the Camellia Garden behind and Wisteria Arbor to the side. If you can time your visit for April, when the wisteria is blooming, you're in for a photogenic treat. Farther on is the Tea Garden with its tea house, and the Lower House with its small Zen Garden. There are no plants in this kind of dry garden, only carefully placed stones and raked gravel that are meant to aid contemplation and instill a sense of timeless peace.

Stop in the Cultural Exchange Center, built in the 1990s, to have a look at the various exhibits and exhibitions (as of 2014, it's also an art gallery). This building, like the Moon Viewing House, was built in Japan using pegs instead of nails, and reassembled on the site. It was modeled after a traditional Japanese merchant's house. Behind the center there is a deck with a lovely view of the verdant hills of Silicon Valley.

As you head back toward the main gate, pause and take another look at the peaceful scene that has charmed and inspired visitors for a hundred years. It's still here to enjoy thanks to the garden lovers who have cared for this living treasure.

montalvo arts center

15400 Montalvo Road, Saratoga, CA 95071
montalvoarts.org
Visit in April and May for wisteria and roses; October and
   November for fall foliage

- 📞 (408) 961-5858 (box office)
- 🕐 Grounds open Apr–Sept Mon–Thurs 8am–7pm, Fri–Sun
   9am–5pm; Oct–Mar Mon–Thurs 8am–5pm, Fri–Sun
   9am–5pm. Villa Montalvo open for tours only by prior
   arrangement; docent-led grounds tours by appointment
- $ Admission free to grounds
- 🐕 Dogs on leash, on upper trails only

Landmark estate with Italianate garden, hiking trails, historic house, and arboretum

Unique among California's historic garden estates, Montalvo is a splendid architectural and garden landmark that also happens to be a lauded performing and visual arts center. The 175-acre estate nestled in the hills of Saratoga, about forty-eight miles south of San Francisco, was the country home of James Duval Phelan (1860–1930), a San Francisco native who served three terms as the city's mayor and two as U.S. senator from California. Phelan bequeathed the property with its Italianate villa and sculpture-filled gardens to Santa Clara County for use as a park and forum for the arts. South Bay residents flock here to enjoy summer outdoor concerts and hiking in the wooded hills. Garden lovers can stroll through a series of refreshed heritage gardens and enjoy one of Northern California's most celebrated landscapes.

Phelan's father, an Irish immigrant, made a bundle as a merchant during the Gold Rush and eventually became a banker. James Jr. attended a Jesuit college and studied law at the University of California, Berkeley, before becoming a banker like his father. He then went into politics. Somewhere along the way he fell in love with the one thing California didn't have much of in those days: art. Nor did California have an identifiable style. Houses and gardens on the East Coast and in Europe served as models for grand houses and gardens in the aspiring West. Villa Montalvo, completed in 1912, is a sturdy Italianate estate, with a red tile roof, an English-style great lawn, and gardens that evoke Mediterranean gardens in Italy and France.

If you're a historic-house buff, arrange in advance for a tour of the grand and grandiose villa, used today for community events and offices. Otherwise, give yourself about an hour to explore the grounds, longer if you want to take a hike or enjoy a picnic. Thanks to the tireless efforts of volunteers, the grounds and gardens of this century-old estate have been rejuvenated and, in some cases, rethought or reinvented to address the challenges brought on by the California water shortage. In addition to Phelan's collection of European statuary, contemporary sculptures and art installations are sited around the grounds.

James Duval Phelan, a mayor of San Francisco and California senator, built Montalvo in 1912 as his country retreat.

The gardens were planted in the early 1920s when Phelan's political career as a senator was over and he was traveling in Europe. He sent photographs and plans of Italian gardens to his head gardener, George Doeltz. With the help of John McLaren (Golden Gate Park's superintendent), Doeltz created the landscape seen today. Like the great landscape parks of Europe, the grounds were designed as a painterly composition, framing distant vistas with classical architectural elements.

From the terrace of Villa Montalvo, the view flows dramatically downhill to the 1.5-acre Great Lawn with its huge, century-old bunya-bunya pine (*Araucaria bidwillii*) from eastern Australia. The view of the lawn, surrounded by trees and pathways, is channeled into the long, formal symmetry of the Italianate Garden, with a freestanding white stone portico at its far end. A low boxwood border runs along the central axis with white roses planted behind it. The outer perimeter of this walled, gated garden is defined by needle-thin cypresses interspersed with fluffier fruit trees. Have a look at the strange creatures gathered around the fountain in the center of the so-called Love Temple. Four almost-life-size and rather grotesque-looking satyrs stand staring into an empty marble basin where a statue of Venus once stood. The satyrs replace four earlier sculptures that were destroyed in the 1989 earthquake. Although at one time their mouths spouted water, today they are dry-mouthed and appear to be whistling. A nearby white marble statue of an embracing Adam and Eve is definitely more romantic—especially since it's meant to convey their idyllic state before their fall from grace.

Among the many fine new trees planted in the border garden that runs along the southeastern length of the Great Lawn is a winter-flowering Hong Kong orchid tree (*Bauhinia* ×*blakeana*), with striking red, fragrant, orchidlike flowers; a rare Wollemi pine (*Wollemia nobilis*), thought to be extinct until it was discovered in a rainforest in New South Wales in 1994; and three pink trumpet trees (*Handroanthus impetiginosus*) with pale gray trunks and lavender flowers in the spring. There are also persimmons and giant avocado trees.

The new Blue Garden was inspired by the fabulous Blue Garden created by Ganna Walska at Lotusland in Montecito. Centered around a Spanish blue fir (*Abies pinsapo*), it's planted with succulents, shrubs, and trees that have a bluish tinge or hue in their foliage. The Phelan Cactus Garden, originally planted by

Phelan in the 1920s to showcase two ponytail palms (*Beaucarnea recurvata*) and a collection of cacti and succulents, has had to be rethought and replanted because of the shade created by overhanging trees.

The garden areas behind and on the sides of the house are more intimate in scale. Have a look at the beautiful Spanish Courtyard enclosed on three sides by the villa's walls and on the north by a wall with a fountain between twin stairways leading up to the Oval Garden. The courtyard is graced by a freestanding central marble fountain and the plantings around it are as architectural as the space itself: palm grass (*Setaria palmifolia*), pygmy date palms (*Phoenix roebelenii*), and Australian tree ferns (*Cyathea australis*). Now a green lawn surrounded by hydrangeas, wisteria, and roses, the Oval Garden was built in the 1950s on the site of the senator's swimming pool.

A stone-cast mermaid rises from the romantic Mermaid Pond, the surrounding area recently replanted with Queensland poplar (*Homalanthus populneus*), long-leafed yellowwood (*Podocarpus henkelii*), and angel's trumpet (*Brugmansia ×cubensis* 'Charles Grimaldi') to enhance the pond's grottolike atmosphere.

There's much to enjoy at Montalvo, including the Lilian Fontaine Garden Theatre located on a hilly slope behind the villa. This 1,200-seat amphitheater is among the Bay Area's oldest and best outdoor performance venues.

The sculpture *Before the Fall* was brought back from Europe by James Phelan to grace the gardens at Montalvo.

san francisco botanical garden

Strybing Arboretum, near the corner of Ninth Avenue and Lincoln Way in Golden Gate Park, San Francisco, CA 94118
sfbotanicalgarden.org
Visit year-round; April–August for maximum blooms; January–March for magnolias; March–May for California native plants

- 📞 (415) 661-1316
- 🕐 Open daily Mar–Sept 7:30am–6pm; Oct–early Nov 7:30am–5pm (Sun Nov–Jan until 4pm)
- $ Admission fee. Free 7:30–9am daily, free all day second Tues every month, Thanksgiving, Dec 25, Jan 1; free for San Francisco city and county residents; free tours Fri–Sun 2pm at Friend's Gate
- 🚌 Public transportation
- ♿ Arboretum is wheelchair accessible
- 🐕 No dogs

Arboretum and wide-ranging botanical garden within Golden Gate Park

Spring brings vibrant colors to the California Native Garden, part of the San Francisco Botanical Garden.

"Are you here to see the puyas?" the woman at the admissions kiosk asked.

"I don't know," I said. "Am I?"

"Oh yes, you'll definitely want to see the puyas in bloom," she said, circling their location on the map she was about to give me. "And the flannelbush and meadow foam in the California Native Garden are both blooming now, too, and the Pacific iris, of course. Oh, and be sure to check out the pincushion proteas—you'll find them in the South Africa section, just here."

I probably would have found all those blossoming beauties on my own, but her infectious enthusiasm—the enthusiasm all plant lovers share—added to the pleasure of exploring the San Francisco

Botanical Garden (SFBG). The puyas (*Puya alpestris, P. chilensis*), bromeliads from the mountains of Chile, had just thrown up a phalanx of stalks that looked like barbaric weapons with turquoise flowers. I finally got to see why meadow foam (*Limnanthes douglasii*) is called that—huge drifts of these wildflowers once covered California meadows with what looked like cream-colored foam. The bright yellow flowers of California flannelbush (*Fremontodendron californicum*) and the small Pacific iris *Iris douglasiana*, two other California natives, were once common sights. Pincushion proteas (*Leucospermum cordifolium*)—with their leathery, evergreen leaves and dense, brightly colored inflorescences with protruding, pinlike styles—thrived in a variety of habitats in Zimbabwe and South Africa. All these and many of the other botanical treasures in the SFBG are now being pushed out of their native habitats, sacrificed on the concrete altar of development. So to see them in full glorious bloom, even if they are a long way from home, is a joy.

Turquoise-hued puyas indigenous to the mountains of Chile bloom in the San Francisco Botanical Garden.

We can thank a woman about whom we know practically nothing for this wide-ranging treasure trove in the heart of San Francisco. William Hammond Hall, who laid out the original features of Golden Gate Park in 1870, included a botanical garden in his plans, but there was no money to develop it. The 55-acre site in the southeastern section of the park sat unused, untended, and unfunded until 1926. That was the year Helene Strybing died and left the bulk of her estate to establish an arboretum primarily for the display of native plants in Golden Gate Park. It took another decade before the funds became available. By that time, the Great Depression was in full depressing swing. But by combining Mrs. Strybing's bequest with government-funded WPA work crews, Hall's botanical garden finally became a reality. Strybing Arboretum opened to the public in 1940.

So who was Helene Strybing? She was born Frederike Sophie Helene Jordan in 1845 in Helstorf, a small town near Hannover, Germany, where her father was an evangelical Lutheran pastor. Helene emigrated to San Francisco where she met and married Christian H. Strybing (born Struebing), a fellow German immigrant who'd come to San Francisco around the time of the Gold Rush. Christian, almost twenty-five years older than Helene, made a fortune as a grocer and then as an importer and seller of tobacco, alcohol, and German-made wine and clothing. When he died in 1895, Helene became a wealthy widow. Thirty-one years later, when she died of heart failure at age eighty-one, Helene left money for memorial church windows in San Francisco and Germany, for her three sisters in Germany, and for various charitable organizations.

But Golden Gate Park got most of her estate (estimated in 1939 to be worth $200,000).

Helene's desire to establish an arboretum in her husband's name (they had no children) came with a further request: that the arboretum display medicinal plants regardless of their place of origin. That opened up a whole new range of botanical possibilities, and it's why this area, now called the San Francisco Botanical Garden at Strybing Arboretum, is home to more than 8,000 different kinds of plants from around the world. Give yourself a couple of hours if you want to stroll through the entire garden at a leisurely pace. Pick up a map at the admissions kiosk to see all the seasonal highlights.

The main gate opens onto the Great Meadow, with Fountain Plaza beyond. These grassy areas are surrounded by a host of collections arranged geographically. Temperate Asia occupies the southeast corner of the garden and stretches northwest to become the Mesoamerican Cloud Forest. Paths lead from the broad leafy walkways to the Bamboo and Dwarf Conifer Ponds. Many of the trees in the garden's magnificent magnolia collection are found in this area; they flower from January through March. The magnolia serves as the signature flower of the SFBG, and the magnolia collection—a hundred strong—is the most significant outside of China. Adjoining this area to the southwest is the Arthur L. Menzies Garden of California Native Plants, a must-see in the spring when a host of wildflowers, shrubs, and trees bursts into colorful bloom. Just beyond is the Redwood Grove, where the giants of California forests rise in somber majesty above a stream.

Continuing in a clockwise direction, you come to the Succulent Garden, where rock steps lead you into a world of bromeliads (those puyas are also called Chilean rock bromeliads), needle-tipped agaves, aloes, and thorny, spiky cacti.

The dense canopy of trees in the Southeast Asian Cloud Forest plays host to epiphytic ferns and plants that live on moisture from dripping leaves and the fogs of San Francisco. The Moon Viewing Garden pays homage to the landscape style and plants of Japan. East of it is the lovely Camellia Garden, another springtime delight.

Along the northern perimeter of the garden are plants from the Andean cloud forest and two of the world's other Mediterranean-climate zones, Australia and South Africa. Other specialty gardens include the Ancient Plant Garden, the Rhododendron Garden, and the Garden of Fragrance constructed in 1965 using stones from a thirteenth-century Spanish monastery; they were purchased by newspaper mogul William Randolph Hearst, who apparently had no use for them at his California castle in San Simeon. The stones have also been used for rock walls, steps, and terraces elsewhere in the garden.

If you're visiting in the spring, keep an eye out for the big pink flowers of the tea trees (*Leptospermum*) growing around the central fountain. The many century-old tea trees (aka manukas) that grow here were imported from Australia by John McLaren, William Hammond Hall's successor as park superintendent, and planted under Monterey pines and cypresses to help stabilize the sand dunes that once covered the western side of the park. For centuries the Maoris of New Zealand used these shrubs as medicinal plants to treat various ailments. The Pacific explorer Captain Cook named the plants tea trees when he learned that drinking a tea made from their leaves warded off scurvy. Helene Strybing, who wanted medicinal plants, regardless of their origin, to be a part of the arboretum she funded, would have been pleased by the bee-friendly tea trees planted around the fountain. But she never would have imagined that one day the most beautiful of them would be named for her: *L. scoparium* 'Helen Strybing'.

You can enjoy a view of the high, green hills around San Pablo Reservoir en route to the Regional Parks Botanic Garden in the East Bay.

east bay

ruth bancroft garden

1552 Bancroft Road, Walnut Creek, CA 94598
ruthbancroftgarden.org
Visit year-round; January–March for cacti and succulent
    blooms

....

📞 (925) 944-9352
🕐 Open Mon–Fri 10am–4pm, Sat 10am–1pm
$ Admission fee
🐕 No dogs

Storied botanical garden by a dryscaping pioneer; specializes in succulents

It always amazes me when I find an extraordinary garden hidden away in an otherwise unassuming residential neighborhood. The Ruth Bancroft Garden is a case in point. Located in Walnut Creek, a well-heeled suburban enclave about twenty-five miles east of San Francisco, this is a truly remarkable garden. It does have a bit of street presence, but you could drive right by and never know the treasures to be found within.

This jewel box of a garden occupies a small portion of what was once a 400-acre walnut and pear farm. The farm was founded in the 1880s by historian and publisher Hubert Howe Bancroft on land that was originally open grassland studded with enormous valley oak trees. Bancroft's collection of Western history formed the basis for the famed Bancroft Library at UC Berkeley.

Ruth Petersson, the force behind this very special garden, was born in 1908, grew up in Berkeley, and studied architecture at UC Berkeley. The stock market crash of 1929 prompted her to reconsider her employment options, and she got a teaching degree instead. For several years she taught home economics at a Merced high school. When she was thirty-one, she married Phillip Bancroft, Jr., Hubert Bancroft's grandson, and moved to the Bancroft farm in Walnut Creek. One might say that was when Ruth Petersson Bancroft became a gardener.

Ruth Bancroft created striking juxtapositions of cacti, succulents, and trees.

She'd always been interested in plants, but now she had some earth to play with—the greatest joy for any gardener. She immediately set about creating a large English-style garden around the main farmhouse. Her plant palette at that time was a fairly traditional mix of roses, perennials, herbs, and bearded iris. And then in the 1950s she bought a potted aeonium. If you're a plant collector, you'll understand how buying an aeonium can change your life. Ruth Bancroft fell in love with succulents and started to collect and grow them in one-gallon pots in her lath house.

Meanwhile, as the years rolled on, Walnut Creek grew and the farm shrank. In 1971, the last of the old walnut orchards was cut down and sold. Phil Bancroft retained 3.5 acres and presented this parcel to his wife so she could create an entirely new garden.

In her sixties and with thirty years of gardening experience, Ruth jumped at the chance. This was a once-in-a-lifetime opportunity to create something really unique: a dry garden focused on drought-tolerant succulents and cacti, with palm trees thrown in for good measure. She hired Lester Hawkins of Western Hill Nursery to help design the layout and planting beds for her collection, which by then numbered in the hundreds and was still mostly being grown in one-gallon pots. Tons of crushed rock and gravel were trucked in to loosen up the heavy alluvial soil and to create mounded planting beds. When you walk through the garden you won't see edging of any kind. It's not an entirely naturalistic landscape, but it works as an artful way to group, display, and contrast the size, texture, form, and color of different plants.

Ruth Bancroft planted for visual appeal rather than by scientific family or geography. There are, for example, several different *Aloe* species planted around the garden, most of them from Africa and the rocky slopes of the Arabian peninsula. *Aloe rubroviolacea* from Saudi Arabia and northern Yemen has thick blue-green leaves and spectacular red flowers. The fall-blooming *A. vacillans* is from the same region and also has vivid flowers of yellow or red. *Aloe elegans*, a native of Ethiopia and Eritrea, has silvery blue foliage and yellow and red flowers. Another fall bloomer is the richly colored *A. fosteri* from South Africa, a spotted aloe with reddish brown teeth, blue-green leaves with creamy dots and striations, and tall, dark purple racemes covered with deep orange and yellow flowers. With its sharp, red-tinged teeth along the margins of sky-blue leaves, *A. glauca* from South Africa looks like it's ready to snap your hand off if you get too close to examine those pretty pink flowers. These large, dramatic aloes make that little aloe vera plant you're growing in your kitchen window look pretty wimpy.

The excellent self-guided tour book available at the visitor center will direct you to all the botanical wonders and rarities to be seen in this intriguing and entertaining garden. How about that blue-gray *Agave franzosinii* near the entrance? When it's ready to perform, it sends up a flower stalk as high as 25 feet—then dies. Or how about those tree-form yuccas with the daggerlike leaves rising directly from the trunk? In their native habitats, these plants have evolved an amazing reproductive strategy: a specialized group of moths takes pollen from one flower, rolls it into a ball, deposits the pollen onto the stigma of another yucca plant flower, then lays eggs in that flower's ovary; the seeds that form as a result feed the

Trithrinax campestris, from northern Argentina and Uruguay, is a fall-flowering beauty at the Ruth Bancroft Garden.

larva of the moth and produce fruit on the plant, thus ensuring the survival of both. *Hesperoyucca whipplei*, distinguished by its striking orb of swordlike blue-gray leaves, is called Our Lord's candle because of the plume of white flowers it sends heavenward.

Though yuccas, agaves, aloes, sedums (stonecrops), and sempervivums (hens and chicks) are the most heavily represented plants, the trees interspersed throughout the garden are equally fascinating and provide some needed shade during the hot summer months. The snow gum tree (*Eucalyptus pauciflora*) is a rare cold-hardy eucalyptus with a ghostly pale trunk streaked with yellow. Torrey pines like the multi-trunked specimen here are

A towering trio of *Washingtonia robusta* trees, California's only native palm, resides at the Ruth Bancroft Garden.

endangered in their native habitat of the Channel Islands. The Chilean wine palm (*Jubaea chilensis*), harvested to near extinction for its sap (which is fermented and made into wine), is now protected in its native Chile. Two unusual trees with long, streaming fountains of leaves look remarkably similar but belong to different plant families and come from different continents. One is a Mexican grass tree (*Dasylirion longissimum*) and the other is an Australian grass tree (*Xanthorrhoea preissii*). Close to the tall, single-leaf pinyon (*Pinus monophylla*) from Nevada is a gnarled bristlecone pine (*P. aristata*), which can live for 5,000 years and is among the planet's oldest living organisms. Among all these exotics, the grand old English oak (*Quercus robur*) and golden locust (*Robinia pseudoacacia* 'Frisia') from the eastern United States look decidedly incongruous. But that trio of giant Washington fan palms (*Washingtonia robusta*), the only palm native to the western United States, looks right at home.

Near the Victorian-looking pavilion known as Ruth's Folly—built in 1972 and part of the enclosed Winter House—is a dramatic display of golden barrel cacti (*Echinocactus grusonii*), now critically endangered in their native habitat in Mexico because of dam building. Other cacti found here are prickly pears (*Opuntia*), silky haired *Oreocereus*, and the multi-branched candelabra cactus (*Cereus*).

Before you leave, have a look at the massive old valley oak (*Quercus lobata*) standing sentinel near the garden entrance. It was here in the 1880s when Hubert Bancroft cleared the land for his walnut and pear orchards. That was almost a hundred years before Ruth Bancroft turned what was left of Hubert's farm into this exquisite garden. And by the way, the Ruth Bancroft Garden was the first garden recognized by the Garden Conservancy as a unique American garden worth preserving and protecting.

berkeley rose garden

Heritage rose garden considered
one of the best in the West,
with more than 200 species

1200 Euclid Avenue, Berkeley, CA 94708
ci.berkeley.ca.us
Visit May–September

....

📞 (510) 981-6660
🕐 Open daily dawn to dusk
$ Admission free
♿ Steep paths may be difficult for wheelchairs and those
   with limited mobility
🚌 Public transportation
🐕 No dogs

A WPA project from the 1930s, the Berkeley Rose Garden is a local landmark in the East Bay.

If ever there was a heritage rose garden worth preserving and restoring, it's this historic gem nestled in the Berkeley Hills northeast of downtown. It has the distinctive Arts and Crafts look of Old Berkeley, the Berkeley of Julia Morgan and Bernard Maybeck, whose architectural aesthetic informed so much campus and residential architecture in the first three decades of the twentieth century. In fact, it was Maybeck who suggested the design for the curved loggia at the top of the garden.

Built during the Great Depression, the Berkeley Rose Garden was an early civic project of the WPA. It opened to the public in 1937 after four years of planning and construction, and it has remained an "in-the-know" destination and Berkeley landmark ever since. Over the decades, the garden has gone through periods of neglect and disrepair. Deer ate so many of the roses that a new perimeter fence had to be installed in the 1990s. The group Friends of the Berkeley Rose Garden is working to revitalize this historic landmark but is hampered by lack of funds and dwindling volunteers.

This is one of those gardens that doesn't require a lot of explanation. It speaks for itself. The small, newly created entry plaza, with its stone balustrade overlooking the garden and distant views of San Francisco Bay, is a favorite spot for Berkeleyites to hang out, and a perfect photo op for visitors. A rose-lined ramp leads you down from the plaza to a 220-foot-long semicircular redwood loggia that runs the length of the garden. Paths below the loggia descend into what is essentially an amphitheater of roses. It's like entering a theater from the uppermost row in the balcony. The amphitheater is divided into two tiers of semicircular rose beds that funnel down the slope and end at a small splashing fountain

(where the theater stage would be) that empties into Strawberry Creek, the stream that runs through the Berkeley campus.

The roses, about 3,000 of them representing a couple hundred species, are planted in terraced beds with beautiful stonework walls that add to the garden's Arts and Crafts appeal. The walls and paths are covered with flowering groundcovers and tiny sedums that stay green year-round. But once the roses start to bloom in May, the garden turns into a showstopping display of color.

I don't want to dissuade you from visiting this garden, but I have to be honest. The roses are well cared for and still put on a magnificent show, but on my last visit, the garden was looking

Sedums planted in the rock walls add to the charm of the Berkeley Rose Garden.

frayed around the edges and in need of maintenance work. Some of the paving stones in the pathways were cracked and the deteriorating loggia was fenced off, hopefully awaiting repair. It's always heartbreaking to see once-grand historic gardens like this turning shabby and unkempt due to lack of funds and civic pride. If the city of Berkeley can't afford to maintain this historic treasure, you'd think a local multi-millionaire might consider ponying up the money.

A tunnel beneath Euclid Avenue connects the garden to Codornices Park, a hillside haven with lovely walks through a woodland filled with oaks, California bays, and redwoods.

blake garden

70 Rincon Road, Kensington, CA 94707
blakegarden.ced.berkeley.edu
Visit year-round

- 📞 (510) 524-2449
- 🕐 Open Mon–Fri 8am–4:30pm; closed university holidays
- $ Admission free
- 🚌 Public transportation
- ♿ Some hilly paths unsuitable for wheelchairs and those with limited mobility
- 🐕 Dogs on leash

Estate turned outdoor classroom, focused on landscape architecture and environmental design

I doubt if the University of California presidents who once called this hilltop estate home ever got as excited about compost as the students who use it now. Composting is hot—literally—at the Blake Garden, as are organic, sustainable gardening practices of all kinds. What began life as a rather rarefied house and garden for the wealthy Blake family of Berkeley is now a 10.5-acre outdoor classroom for students studying landscape architecture and environmental design at UC Berkeley. What makes the place fascinating is its juxtaposition of different gardening elements, styles, and ideas spanning several decades.

The influential landscape architect and writer Garrett Eckbo created this simple pergola, now in the Blake Garden, in 1973.

Located four miles north of the Berkeley campus, in the town of Kensington, the Blake Garden sits on a windy hilltop with memorable views of San Francisco Bay and Golden Gate Bridge. It's fairly close to the Berkeley Rose Garden, so you easily combine a visit to both.

When their house in Berkeley was earmarked for a new sports stadium, Anson Blake and his wife Anita bought twenty-two acres in nearby (and almost completely undeveloped) Kensington. Anson, the son of a Gold Rush–era pioneer, was in the rock,

paving, and quarry business and had looked at this property as
a quarry site. But where Anson saw rocks (specifically glauco-
phane schist with seams of serpentine), Anita saw a landscape that
encapsulated a bit of Northern California's diverse terrain. The
Blakes moved into their elegant new Spanish Colonial Revival
house in 1924 and remained there for the rest of their lives. They
bequeathed the house and ten acres to UC Berkeley for use as the
president's house. It was used for that purpose from 1967 to 2009
and is now a teaching facility and outdoor laboratory for UC
Berkeley's Department of Landscape Architecture and Environmental Design.

Both Anson and Anita were graduates of UC Berkeley, and
Anita's sister, Mabel Symmes, was one of the first female graduates of the UC Berkeley Department of Landscape Architecture. Women back then found it almost impossible to establish

professional careers in a field that was so dominated by men, so Mrs. Blake enlisted her sister to plan the gardens around the new house. You can see the architectural bones of the original formal garden in front of the Blake house. A rustic stonework stairway descends from the terrace above to a long reflecting pool with a grotto at the end. The pool was meant to capture some of the water that drained down from the hills above. Planted around it was the Pink Garden—only remnants remain—with pink-flowering shrubs and trees.

The house, unfortunately, has not only been in decline for some time, it's been in a literal slide. The whole area is smack-dab on top of the Hayward Fault, and the house is moving downhill a fraction of an inch every year, disturbing foundations and cracking walls and ceilings. It now sits empty, awaiting its fate.

Mabel Symmes's garden design is fairly sensitive to the property's hilly terrain, with its streams and rocky outcroppings. To the right of the house, head down the hill into the imposing Redwood Grove. Anson Blake, whose business was rocks, no doubt had a say in hiring the expert stonemasons who built and embedded the rustic stone stairs, benches, and pools in the grove. The redwoods came from the Blakes' property in Berkeley. A few other trees and shrubs also remain from the Blake era, most of them located around the house. The rest of the garden has seen many changes, however, and continues to evolve and be transformed by class projects. The emphasis now is on drought-tolerant plants and environmental sustainability, concepts that weren't so important back in the Blakes' era.

The groomed formality of the garden around the house gives way to a more natural landscape on the rest of the hillside. Students have identified over 1,300 plant species over the years, many of them native or introduced since the 1960s. Getting rid of invasive plants is an ongoing process. From the Redwood Grove you can follow a winding path through the dry, hilly terrain with its schist outcroppings and woodland areas. The California Native Grass area gives you an idea of the kinds of tough, drought-tolerant needlegrasses (*Nassella*) and wild ryes (*Leymus*) that covered much of California's grasslands before the introduction of showier exotic grasses from elsewhere. In a wetter part of the hillside, California tule grass—used for centuries by native Ohlone tribes for basket weaving—has been planted.

An open-sided tunnel snaking down a hillside is part of the kid-friendly Create with Nature area at Blake Garden.

It might not look like much, but that simple little wooden pergola covered with vines was designed by preeminent landscape architect Garrett Eckbo (1910–2000). Eckbo's 1950 book *Landscape for Living* is one of the seminal texts for modern ideas about landscape architecture. The pergola was built for the 1973 San Francisco Flower and Garden Show, stored here (Eckbo was head of UC Berkeley's Department of Landscape Architecture from 1963 to 1969), and eventually reconstructed. It fits beautifully and unobtrusively into the hillside landscape, a modernist accompaniment to those rustic stone benches, steps, and pools built in the 1920s.

Continue on and you'll come to the Mediterranean Garden, where the gorgeous view vies with the plantings. Look nearby for a massive coast live oak—it's an original native tree. The eucalyptus and acacia trees in Quarry Hollow, or Australian Hollow, were placed by Anita Blake nearly a century ago.

In keeping with the garden's commitment to sustainability, all cut and fallen woody material throughout the property is recycled. And what better way to do that than by adopting the Scandinavian recycling method known as *Hügelkultur*, in which you compost the wood by burying it beneath a mound of earth. You'll see the mound near an area called The Lookout, where the air is scented by California bay laurels and there's a view of Mt. Tamalpais in the distance. From here, as you head up the trail toward the garden's top ridge, you'll also pass an intriguing tunnel-like struc-

ture made out of branches snaking down the hillside. It's part of the Create with Nature area for kids. Finally, you're back up at the Event Lawn, near the entrance, where graduation ceremonies and special events take place. The lawn was originally twice the size it is now. Instead of grass, drought-tolerant plants have been planted around the margins.

I wouldn't expect anyone but the most ardent gardeners to check out the composting area near the classroom building. The school uses both worm and hot composting methods to create ultra-rich organic soil. I have a feeling that Mabel Symmes would approve.

forrest deaner native plant botanic garden

A colorful introduction to the state's spectacular array of native plants

The orange berries of a golden currant add brilliant color to the fall palette at Forrest Deaner Native Plant Botanic Garden.

Benicia State Recreation Area, Benicia, CA 94510
bsragarden.dreamhosters.com
Visit March–June for maximum blooms

⏰ Open daily 8am–sunset
$ Admission fee to enter Benicia State Recreation Area
🐕 Dogs on leash

If you're out exploring Solano County northeast of San Francisco, I would encourage you to pay a visit to the Forrest Deaner Native Plant Botanic Garden, about 1.5 miles from the historic town of Benicia. It's relatively small, relatively new, and run entirely by volunteers. But this garden packs a lot of botanical punch into its 3.5 acres, and it will only get better with age.

The garden seems larger than it is, thanks in part to the expansive landscape that surrounds it. It was created within Benicia State Recreation Area, a park located on Southampton Bay between the Carquinez Strait and a ridge of low, grassy hills (visually marred by a telephone tower). It's an ecologically important area where fourteen tributaries of the Sacramento and San Joaquin Rivers flow into the strait and make their way to the Pacific. If you're a birder, bring your binoculars.

The garden, started in 2004, is a memorial to Forrest Deaner, a California-born journalist who wanted to help preserve his state's rapidly disappearing native plants. We should all be so lucky to have a garden like this one dedicated to our memory. It's well planned and maintained and features about 4,000 plants of approximately 300 different species. The garden is divided into different habitat zones and all the plants are labeled.

The Meadow Plant Community showcases different drought-tolerant native grasses, including California fescue (*Festuca californica*) and California buckwheat (*Eriogonum fasciculatum*). Purple needlegrass (*Nassella pulchra*) is the California state grass. Here and elsewhere in the garden you'll find plants that provide food to sustain two kinds of gorgeous butterflies. The giant black pipevine swallowtail feeds on the foliage of California Dutchman's pipe (*Aristolochia californica*) and monarch butterflies feed on showy milkweed (*Asclepias speciosa*). You'll see more grasses in the Hummingbird-Butterfly-Native American Garden. Deergrass (*Muhlenbergia rigens*) was woven into baskets by native tribes and dyed with extracts from western redbuds and black oak bark. The Chaparral Plant Community bursts into springtime color when California flannelbush (*Fremontodendron californicum*) opens its bright yellow blossoms and the branches of coast silk tassel (*Garrya elliptica*) are draped with a spectacular show of long pendent flowers. This is where you'll find native shrubs like elderberry, long used to make wine and a digestive tea, toyons, manzanitas, mountain mahogany, and California currants and gooseberries (both favorites with hummingbirds), as well as California sagebrush and rabbitbrush, both members of the aster family. The Coastal Sage Scrub area is home to dwarf coyote bush, coyote mint, common snowberry, spice bush, coffeeberry, foothill penstemon, and oceanspray. The herblike scents that rise from these plants after a winter rain are intoxicating.

The garden contains a small but interesting collection of native oak trees. Blue oaks (*Quercus douglasii*), once common in the California Coast Ranges, are named for the dark blue-green tint of their leaves. Valley oaks (*Q. lobata*), endemic to interior valleys and foothills, grow into some of the largest and longest-lived oaks, but they require a year-round source of groundwater.

And speaking of water, once you've explored the garden, head down to the marshes around Southampton Bay. They're part of a rare and endangered wetlands area and a great spot for birdwatching. You might spy Virginia rails, black rails, and endangered California clapper rails hiding in the marsh vegetation, or see egrets, pelicans, and terns diving into the bay. Suisun song sparrows and saltmarsh common yellowthroats sing in the cottonwoods and other trees in the park. The plants, birds, and butterflies are lovely reminders of the richness of California's native flora and fauna—and the importance of preserving them for future generations.

Swarms of monarch and swallowtail butterflies visit the Forrest Deaner Native Plant Botanic Garden to feed on the showy milkweed.

morcom amphitheater of roses

700 Jean Street, Oakland, CA 94610
oaklandnet.com (Office of Parks and Recreation)
Visit mid-May–September

- 📞 (510) 597-5039
- 🕐 Open daily 7am–8pm
- $ Admission free
- 🐕 No dogs

A graceful, eighty-year-old bowl of heirloom roses in Oakland's Piedmont section

The Morcom Amphitheater of Roses (the name is a nod to the garden's scooped design) is a charming period piece of a garden, carved out of a ravine in the Grand Lake neighborhood of Oakland. The locals love it but it doesn't have quite enough oomph to make it a major garden destination, so I'm combining it with two other Oakland gardens: the Kaiser Center Roof Garden and the grounds of the Oakland Museum of California, both created in the 1960s. You can visit all three of these refreshing Oakland landscapes in half a day.

The eighty-year-old amphitheater of roses can be seen in half an hour, and that includes sniffing and photo op time. The city of Oakland acquired these seven acres of land in 1911 for use as a public space. Topographically, it's a natural declivity, like a small valley, folded into the ridge that runs like a spine through the city's Piedmont section. Nothing was done to the property until 1932, when the WPA constructed a formal garden to highlight heirloom rose varieties. The idea for the garden came from the Oakland Businessmen's Breakfast Club. One of its members, a landscape architect with the unfortunate name of Arthur Cobbledick, designed the garden's landscape features. Oakland mayor Fred Morcom planted the first rose in 1933.

Though the garden is formal, it has a romantic quality that allies it to the Arts and Crafts movement popular in the Bay Area in the early twentieth century. The Berkeley Rose Garden is also an amphitheater built in this style. Morcom features a long rectangular area with an oval-shaped central lawn flanked by a Classical-style pavilion on one side and, on the other, tiered rose beds with a water feature that cascades down to a reflecting pool in the center of the lawn. Beyond the lawn, a walkway called The Mother's Walk, planted with rose trees, leads to the Florentine Oval, another series of formal, geometrically shaped rose beds. From here, stairways rise to the Oakland Avenue entrance above. Winding pathways encircle these primary areas and lead into parts of the surrounding wooded hillsides.

The Morcom Amphitheater of Roses is planted in a seven-acre natural valley.

Over fifty years old, the Kaiser Center Roof Garden brings nature to the top of a parking garage in the Lake Merritt–Uptown section of Oakland.

Kaiser Center Roof Garden

I've tried in this book to open up the idea of "garden" to include all kinds of interesting outdoor spaces from different eras. The Kaiser Center Roof Garden (300 Lakeside Drive, Oakland, CA 94612; open free to public Mon–Fri 8am–5pm) is an intriguing 3.5-acre garden built atop a five-story parking structure adjacent to Kaiser Tower in the Lake Merritt–Uptown section of Oakland. This rooftop garden is a classic example of midcentury modern design. The 28-story Kaiser Tower, designed by Welton Becket and constructed in 1960 as steel magnate Henry Kaiser's corporate headquarters and residence, is another classic of the age. The rooftop garden was built a couple years later. If only all ugly parking structures were blessed with a rooftop garden as nice as this one. It's not the most imaginative landscaping you'll ever see—in fact, it has a kind of smooth corporate veneer that fits in with the aesthetics of the era. But where else can you step out of a parking garage elevator to find yourself on a rooftop with an asymmetrical reflecting pool (so 1960s) spanned by a low wooden bridge, surrounded by an expansive green lawn bordered by mature trees and shrubs? The garden is enlivened by beds of bright annuals and looks out over Lake Merritt, the Oakland hills, and the distant skyline of San Francisco. This garden is probably of more interest to landscape architects and urban gardeners than it is to those who like their gardens planted firmly in the earth. But if I worked in a hermetically sealed high-rise office tower in this area, I know where I'd escape to on my lunch hour.

Oakland Museum of California

Another icon of the 1960s, located within walking distance of the Kaiser Center Roof Garden, the Oakland Museum of California (1000 Oak Street, Oakland, CA 94607; museumca.org; admission fee; open Wed–Sun) is full of surprises. Architects come to pay homage to Kevin Roche's landmark of Brutalist architecture built in three set-back tiers with large glass windows facing a central courtyard. Art lovers come to enjoy the world's most comprehensive and historically important collection of California art. And if you're a garden lover or landscape architect, you'll no doubt be drawn outside to explore the rooftop gardens created in 1967–68 by landscape architects Dan Kiley and Geraldine Knight Scott. Planting the terraces and central courtyard of this massive concrete structure was a formidable challenge, to say the least. Kiley and Knight Scott wanted to achieve a kind of enclosed Roman villa look, using olive and cedar trees, trellised and hanging bougainvillea vines, and fragrant herbs and flowers to soften the hard concrete shell of the building. Time, nature, and inadequate funding have now, unfortunately, taken a toll on their ambitious work of landscape art. Within the intricate multi-level maze of terraces, stairways, and paths, along the perimeter walls and within the courtyards, you can still get a ghostly glimpse of the garden that was meant to be an integral part of this important museum's inner and outer environment. Imagine if the grounds here were once again seen as a canvas for a garden that was not just a setting for art, but a major work of art itself. It could be as exciting as Robert Irwin's garden at the Getty Center in Los Angeles or the High Line in New York—and a major tourist draw for Oakland and the museum.

The terraced gardens and central lawn of the Oakland Museum of California overlook Lake Merritt.

regional parks botanic garden and tilden nature area

Historic site now devoted exclusively to California's native trees, shrubs, grasses, and wildflowers

Intersection of Wildcat Canyon Road and South Park Drive, Berkeley, CA 94708
nativeplants.org
Visit year-round; April–June for wildflowers and ceanothus

....

📞 (510) 544-3169 or (888) 327-2757
🕐 Open daily 8:30am–5pm
$ Admission free; free guided tours Fri–Sat 11am and 2pm
🚌 Public transportation
♿ Some steep paths and stairs are unsuitable for wheelchairs and those with limited mobility
🐕 No dogs

We can thank the citizens of Alameda County for the 754 acres of forested parkland in the hills above Berkeley. In 1934, to protect the area from impending development, they voted to create Tilden Park and the country's first regional park district.

The area had been home to the Huchiun Ohlone indigenous peoples centuries before Berkeley was founded in 1868. The Native Americans lived along what was later called Wildcat Creek. The hunter-gatherer Ohlones were displaced by the Spanish and Mexicans, who created ranches and dairy farms. When California officially came into U.S. hands, and tens of thousands of new settlers began pouring into the region during the Gold Rush, the land and waters of Wildcat Creek were claimed for other uses.

But more and more water was needed to keep California growing, and eventually the Sierra Nevada was tapped to become the state's primary water supply. After that, local watersheds like Wildcat Creek ceased to have the same importance and the hills behind Berkeley were opened up for development. If the East Bay residents hadn't organized to create Tilden Park, you would see nothing but houses and commercial and university development in the Berkeley Hills today.

Within Tilden Park, a few minutes from the University of California Botanical Garden at Berkeley, you'll find the Regional Parks Botanic Garden. Established in 1940, it's not nearly as big or as comprehensive as Berkeley's world-class botanic garden, but if you're a garden lover, you'll want to check it out. It's devoted exclusively to California's native trees, shrubs, grasses, and wildflowers. The landscaping, done by the Civilian Conservation Corps (CCC) over seventy-five years ago, adds to its charm. Keep in mind that the garden's winding pathways and sometimes steep rock stairways (without handrails) were created long before ADA

A grove of coast redwoods lends a solemn majesty to Regional Parks Botanic Garden.

requirements were in place. That said, anyone with reasonably good mobility won't have a problem exploring this interesting garden.

The entrance, through a gate in cyclone fencing, isn't exactly glamorous, but if the fencing wasn't there, there would be no garden. The deer would eat everything in sight except perhaps the thorny cacti and succulents you'll find just inside the entrance.

You can easily explore this compact garden in an hour or so. The paths wind through Wildcat Creek canyon, passing areas that showcase plant communities representative of California's incredibly diverse terrain—from the High Sierras and Coast Ranges to the northern rainforests, the southern deserts, and the Channel Islands.

The garden, as you might expect, is loaded with native species of manzanita and California lilac (*Ceanothus*), some of them deliciously fragrant. There's an impressively solemn grove of coast redwoods and a lovely stand of alders, their leaves a shimmering yellow canopy in the fall.

After you leave the garden, head over to the Tilden Nature Area in the northern section of the park. From 1935 to 1941 this was the site of a CCC camp. The men built the roads, shelters, and picnic sites in use today. Skilled stonemasons created the distinctive stonework used in the buildings. If you have kids in tow, they'll love the carousel and petting zoo at Little Farm, a red wooden barn built in 1955 by carpentry students from Berkeley high schools. You can pick up a trail guide at the Environmental Education Center and hike for miles in the surrounding forest.

The Regional Parks Botanic Garden features California native flora, much of it now rare or endangered.

university of california botanical garden at berkeley

200 Centennial Drive, Berkeley, CA 94720; pay-to-park lot
across the street
botanicalgarden.berkeley.edu
Visit year-round; April–July for maximum blooms

....

📞 (510) 643-2755
🕐 Open daily 9am–5pm; closed first Tuesday of the month, Thanksgiving, Dec 25, Jan 1
$ Admission fee; free first Wednesday of the month, free docent-led tours Thursday–Sunday and first Wednesday of the month at 1:30pm
🚌 Public transportation
♿ Some paths may be difficult for wheelchairs
🐕 No dogs

Spring visitors to the University of California Botanical Garden at Berkeley are greeted by colorful perennials.

The state's largest botanical garden and an official plant rescue center, filled with rare and endangered global species

Berkeley is not lacking in gardens to visit, but if you want to be wowed by all-out plant power, put the University of California Botanical Garden at Berkeley (UCBG) at the top of your list. Located above the campus in Strawberry Canyon, this 34-acre botanical haven contains one of the largest and most diverse plant collections in the country. It's a living museum and like any great museum, it's a place where you can wander happily for hours and discover new and rare surprises at every turn.

The garden celebrated its 125th anniversary in 2015. It was officially founded in 1890, but its antecedents go back as far as 1870, when a small research collection of "economic plants" was started on the Berkeley campus under the aegis of the university's Department of Agriculture. In 1890, the garden became part of the Department of Botany and moved to another campus location. Its goal at that time was to form a living collection of the native trees, shrubs, and herbaceous plants of California and surrounding states. But the garden, like the population of California, just kept growing. In the 1920s it moved to its present location in Strawberry Canyon and began to enlarge its scope, acquiring plants from all over the world and organizing them according to their geographical origins, in settings resembling their native habitats.

There are presently about 9,000 species in cultivation at UCBG, seventy percent of which are wild-collected. Some of the plants are incredibly rare; about 2,000 of them are endangered in their native habitats. So this botanical garden, like others throughout the world, serves as a giant gene bank of biotic diversity. Five hundred to 1,000 new plants are added every year.

Up through the 1960s the garden kept its focus on research and teaching and wasn't much in the public eye. Since the 1970s, however, as all parts of California's once-great free public university system have been defunded and dismantled, the University of California's botanical gardens and arboreta have had to seek more outside support. They are all placing a greater emphasis on fundraising, public outreach, accessibility, and volunteers to help maintain and interpret the collections. The UCBG is no exception, and it has done a remarkable job in opening its outstanding plant collections to the public. The greater your interest in the plants of the world, the more this garden will give back to you. But you can also simply enjoy it for the beauty of its landscaping and views of San Francisco Bay and Golden Gate Bridge.

Enter via the attractive entrance plaza created in 2008. The Water Wise Entry Garden was built in response to the California drought. All the plants you see are suitable for home gardens and require far less water to maintain. Except, that is, for the bog-loving and carnivorous pitcher plants (*Darlingtonia*) that grow in a decorative planter in the center of the plaza.

Julia Morgan Hall, the Arts and Crafts–style building you see down the slope, was designed by iconic California architect Julia Morgan (1872–1957). She designed several notable buildings in Berkeley (as well as Hearst Castle in San Simeon); this hall, now used as a gallery and exhibition space, was moved to the garden in 2014. From the entry plaza you can head out in many different directions. Two greenhouses not far from the entry plaza might be your first or last stop. The Arid House and its associated outdoor plantings contains one of the largest collections of succulents and cacti in the world, with specimens from Bolivia, Peru, Mesoamerica, Australia, New Zealand, and South Africa. You'll also find a large collection of xerophytic ferns that have adapted to arid conditions. Tender tropical ferns, orchids, and carnivorous plants are housed in the second greenhouse. West of here, you'll find the Cycad and Palm Garden.

One of the nation's largest collections of Asian rhododendrons can be found at the University of California Botanical Garden at Berkeley.

The sizzling, spiky world of cacti and deserts turns soft, lush, and green when you enter the Asian collection of hardy plants from Japan, China, and Korea. Over 400 varieties of rhododendrons blossom here from January through June, their colors glowing in the shady understory. A small, serene pond surrounded by hewn rocks and filled with water-loving plants was originally an exhibit at the 1939 World's Fair on Treasure Island in San Francisco Bay. The reconstruction and much of the other construction work in the garden was carried out by the WPA. A newly created Chinese Medicinal Herb Garden is located at the southern end of the Asia section.

Throughout the garden there is an emphasis on plants from the world's five Mediterranean climate zones: California, the

The University of California Botanical Garden at Berkeley saved this specimen of Australian *Xanthorrhoea glauca* in 2003.

Mediterranean Basin, Australia, South Africa, and Chile. Characterized by cool, wet winters and hot, dry summers, these areas foster the growth of a widely diverse group of plants. The Mediterranean, Australasia, South Africa, and South America areas of the garden all feature species of Mediterranean plants.

For the best view of San Francisco Bay and the Golden Gate Bridge, head to the Garden of Old Roses, a specialty garden located on a terrace within the South America section and just below the Mediterranean section. The heirloom roses, a lovely anomaly in this setting otherwise devoted to wild-collected plants, serves as a photogenic foreground to the bay and bridge views. Not surprisingly, this is a popular spot for weddings.

The southwestern section of the garden is dedicated to plants of Mexico and Central America. Part of it is a pine and oak woodland with rare Mexican oaks. Another rare beauty is the Mexican flowering dogwood (*Cornus florida* subsp. *urbiniana*) with flower bracts that, unlike those on other dogwoods, are fused together.

The largest of all the geographic sections, roughly one-third of the garden, is, fittingly, California. The Golden State has more biotic diversity than any other state and is one of twenty-five biodiversity hotspots that account for about forty-four percent of the world's plant species. The California section contains almost a quarter of all the state's identified native plant species, grouped by plant communities. The chaparral section is home to the tough, low-growing, shrubby plants and grasses that were once a common sight in coastal California, but are now disappearing because of development. There are outstanding collections of manzanitas (*Arctostaphylos*), California lilacs (*Ceanothus*), and California bulbous plants in the lily and amaryllis families. Picnic tables are set up in a shady grove of California oaks. What a pleasant way to end your botanical world tour.

sonoma & vicinity

The vineyards seen from the terrace of Ferrari-Carano Winery are part of a Sonoma Valley wine-making tradition that dates back to the 1850s.

marin art and garden center

30 Sir Francis Drake Boulevard, Ross, CA 94957
magc.org
Visit year-round; March–June for roses

- ☎ (415) 455-5260
- ⏲ Open Mon–Sat 9am–5pm; closed holidays
- $ Admission free
- 🐕 Dogs on leash

Community-minded park with heritage trees and eclectic gardens

The new Rose Garden and the old Octagon House at the Marin Art and Garden Center.

There are plenty of scenic spots to enjoy in Marin County. Head north across the Golden Gate Bridge (but not at rush hour) on Highway 101 and you're on your way to the Muir Woods redwood forest, the Marin Headlands, Stinson Beach, Point Reyes National Seashore, and Mt. Tamalpais.

The town of Ross, home to the Marin Art and Garden Center (MAGC), is located about eighteen miles north of San Francisco. This intriguing oasis, with its heritage trees, cache of vintage buildings, and assorted gardens is a microcosm of Marin County history.

If you live in the vicinity you're probably aware of MAGC's many community programs—it's been hosting artistic, cultural, and horticultural events since it was founded in 1945. Before that, the property was part of a private estate called Sunnyside. Before that, it was part of a vast Mexican land grant and called Rancho Punta de Quentin. And before any of that, it was known to the Coast Miwok indigenous peoples, hunter-gatherers who occupied today's Marin County for thousands of years before the Spanish arrived in the late 1700s. This overlay of history, reflected in the parklike grounds and gardens, adds to the pleasure of a visit.

To my mind, a chronological tour of these grounds is more interesting than an entrance-to-exit walk-through—at least in writing. Let's start with the Native Basketry Garden in Redbud Gulch, behind the theater barn. Developed by renowned basketry and plant artist Charles Kennard, this habitat garden is a living history book that shows the kinds of plant materials used by native peoples, including the Coast Miwoks, for making baskets. It was developed around a patch of native Santa Barbara sedge (*Carex barbarae*) and includes flexible-stemmed willows (*Salix*), elderberries (*Sambucus*), western redbud (*Cercis occidentalis*), western leatherwood (*Dirca occidentalis*), grasses, and other plants used for weaving by indigenous tribes for millennia.

Trees can provide a unique link to the past. Take a look at the pear tree growing in front of the Octagon House. It's a graft taken from the last remaining pear tree in the orchard of Mission San Rafael, established in 1817. The Spanish Franciscans founded missions up and down the coast, established the first gardens in California, and introduced the first European fruits, grains, and vegetables. The old pear is one of several fruit trees scattered around the grounds (including orange and apple) adding fragrance in the spring and rich color in the fall (persimmon). Look for them near the Livermore Pavilion and around the edges of the property.

In 1821, following the Mexican War of Independence, the Spanish missions were disbanded and the enormous land grants bestowed by the Spanish crown came into Mexican hands. The land occupied by the MAGC was part of the 8,877-acre Rancho Punta de Quentin. But when the United States took control and California became a state in 1850, the Mexican land grants were up for grabs. James Ross, a liquor merchant from San Francisco, bought a portion of the ranch and settled there in 1857. (The town of Ross is named for him.) His tenure is marked by the presence of the majestic English oak (*Quercus robur*) near the entrance. The tree, one of the largest of its species in the country, was planted in 1860. The garden's oak collection also includes several evergreen coast live oaks (*Q. agrifolia*), white oaks (*Q. alba*), and red oaks (*Q. rubra*).

After Ross's death, George Worn, his business associate, married Ross's daughter Annie. The couple took possession of twenty-two acres of the property—the site that is now the Marin Art and Garden Center—and built a grand house they called Sunnyside. The Worns' tenancy resulted in a small building called the Octagon House, built in 1864, where they lived while Sunnyside was being built. (The building now serves as the Moya Library.) A giant sequoia planted in 1875 also remains from the Worn era. (George and Annie's daughter, Isabella, became a noted horticulturist in the Bay Area and served as the chief gardener at Filoli.)

The Worns' fortunes took a nosedive in 1886, when the silver markets tanked. Sunnyside was sold to Jonathan Kittle and his wife Harriett, twenty years his junior. They doubled the size of the house and lived there with their four children until the house burned down in 1931. Today, a fountain marks the site where the house stood.

After the fire, the property sat unused and derelict until two remarkable women, Caroline Livermore and Gladys Smith, managed to raise funds to acquire and preserve it as a community resource. Livermore and Smith were community activists and conservationists at a time when Marin County was growing rapidly. The Marin Art and Garden Center opened in 1945 and served as the headquarters for several horticultural, cultural, and artistic groups.

The history of the Marin Art and Garden Center stretches back to a time before California's statehood.

With the exception of the Octagon House and the magnificent heritage trees, everything you see here dates from about 1947 onward. There has been an increasing emphasis on ecology, organic gardening techniques, and the use of native and drought-tolerant plants in the ornamental and demonstration garden areas that have been created over the past seventy years. In the Habitat Garden and the Sun Garden you'll find a colorful mix of salvias, milkweed, verbena, goldenrod, coreopsis, matilija poppies, several varieties of California lilac (*Ceanothus*), and more.

The lovely Rose Garden, enclosed within a decorative wrought-iron (deer-proof) fence, was planted in 2004 by the Marin Rose Society. The oldest garden is the Memory Garden, completed in 1953 as a quiet spot for remembrance and reflection. Two statues, *The Reclining Lady* and *The Standing Lady*, grace this peaceful area behind the Octagon House. The Memory Garden seems an apt place to end this tour through time of a place so rich in Marin County history.

luther burbank home and gardens

204 Santa Rosa Avenue, Santa Rosa, CA 95402
lutherburbank.org
Visit year-round; May and June for roses and poppies

....

- 📞 (707) 524-5445
- 🕐 Gardens open daily 8am–dusk; museum open Apr–Oct Tues–Sun 10am–4pm
- $ Admission free
- 🐕 No dogs

A step back in time to the home and gardens of America's greatest plant breeder

You can thank Luther Burbank (or not) for those McDonald's french fries you keep vowing to stop eating. Most of McDonald's fries are made from a potato known as Russet Burbank, a brown-skinned spud that's an offshoot of the Burbank, a potato Luther Burbank developed in 1872. You couldn't patent potatoes back in those pre-Monsanto days, so Burbank sold the rights to his new potato for $150 and used the money to move to California.

It was the smartest business move this pioneering plant breeder ever made. For the rest of his life, Burbank lived in Santa Rosa and carried out his endless and exacting plant experiments in the gardens surrounding his home and at Gold Ridge Farm in nearby Sebastopol.

The Burbank potato made Luther Burbank (1849–1926) famous. But you can also thank him every time you bite into the

Luther Burbank designed this greenhouse as his office and plant laboratory in the 1880s.

sweet strawberry-orange flesh of a Santa Rosa plum, a variety he introduced in 1906. Soon after, he crossed plums and apricots to create the first plumcots. The Royal walnut trees he developed in the 1880s became the standard commercial walnut trees in the country. And how about that white blackberry he created? Burbank was as interested in ornamental flowers as he was in edible fruits, vegetables, nuts, and grains. Those lovely Shasta daisies you grow in a sunny spot in your garden—the ones with the white petals and golden centers—were introduced by Luther Burbank in 1901 after seventeen years of labor.

The list of Luther Burbank's more than 800 plant creations, inventions, innovations, hybrids, novelties, improvements, and introductions is staggering. This transplanted New Englander, a self-taught man who never finished high school, became the most famous horticulturist in the world. He was a household name in pre-supermarket days, when people who grew their own food and flowers were constantly on the lookout—as were farmers, nurserymen, and orchardists—for better-tasting, faster-growing, longer-lasting, and nicer-looking fruits, flowers, and vegetables. Burbank was the rock star of the plant world to them, a cross between a wizard and a saint, a man so revered that his birthday (March 7) is celebrated as Arbor Day in California and trees (probably his own hybrids) are planted in his honor.

Burbank was a plant inventor more than he was an environmentalist. He developed the famous spineless prickly pear cactus (I guess we could call it the prickless pear) as cattle fodder, with the goal of turning the desert into one vast ranch for grazing cattle. That the cattle would destroy entire desert ecosystems apparently didn't concern him. Because here's the thing: every native plant Burbank saw— from the persimmon to the poppy to the

Between 1907 and 1925, Luther Burbank developed over sixty varieties of spineless cacti for possible use as cattle fodder.

cactus—he wanted to "improve" and make "better" or more "useful." He also introduced the Himalayan blackberry that now runs rampant and is the bane of farmers and gardeners everywhere.

That's not to denigrate his achievements, which you'll learn about in fascinating detail on a visit to the Luther Burbank Home and Gardens in Santa Rosa. Some of his more notable creations can be seen in the 1.5-acre garden-park that surrounds the modified Greek Revival house where Burbank lived with his mother and sister from 1884 to 1906. The property, which includes the rather charming greenhouse he designed in 1889 and used as one of his plant laboratories, is a registered National, State, and City Historic Landmark. In 2005, the carriage house was transformed into an attractive museum devoted to Burbank's accomplishments. The grounds include a Wildlife Habitat Garden, an Edible Landscape Garden, and a Medicinal Garden.

But what about Burbank's personal life? The facts we have seem to indicate that it was easier for Burbank to be intimate with plants than with people. He was born in Lancaster, Massachusetts, the thirteenth of eighteen children. His mother and sister moved out to California to be with him and provided much of his emotional sustenance. His first wife was one Helen Coleman from Ohio. Though no one in that tight-lipped age used the term "battered husband," that appears to be what Burbank was. (At one point Helen gave him a black eye.) After divorcing her in 1896 and paying out a big settlement, Burbank remained single until 1916, when he married his secretary, Elizabeth. She was twenty-nine. Elizabeth adored him. Burbank died in 1926, Elizabeth in 1977. She's the one who had the memorial fountain built and who donated the property to the city of Santa Rosa.

If you can, book a docent-led tour that takes you inside the Luther Burbank House. After Burbank's death, Elizabeth moved into this house, where Burbank had once lived with his mother and sister. It's a cozy, charming period piece that instantly transports you back to the age of antimacassars, writing desks, and upright parlor pianos. And it's loaded with Burbank memorabilia—like that famous photograph of Luther Burbank standing with Henry Ford and Thomas Edison: the Big Three inventors of what was fast becoming the modern age. Consider combining your visit here with a trip to nearby Gold Ridge Farm in Sebastopol, where Burbank carried out most of his plant-breeding experiments.

From this window in his foreman's cottage, Luther Burbank could look out at the fields of his experiment farm in Sebastopol.

Gold Ridge Farm

If you're interested in the working methods and botanical offspring of this fascinating plantsman, drive about seven miles west from Santa Rosa to visit Gold Ridge Farm (entrance at 7777 Bodega Avenue, Sebastopol, CA 95472; grounds open daily). This three-acre remnant of Burbank's ten-acre experiment farm still contains trees, flowers, and vines planted by or descended from the ones Burbank planted more than a hundred years ago. For his experiments, he would plant thousands of saplings, sprouts, or seedlings close together in long north-south rows so he could more easily inspect each plant and choose the best for continued work. He bought the land in 1885 and bicycled over every day to propagate, cross-pollinate, hybridize, graft, bud, sprout, and select his plants. Sometimes he would stay overnight in the now-restored foreman's cottage. You can visit the cottage on a docent-led tour, but it's really the gardens you want to see. They're a little ghostly, but they provide a living link to the remarkable achievements of Luther Burbank.

cornerstone sonoma

A gallery of contemporary gardens and the *Sunset* test gardens highlight this upscale retail setting

23570 Highway 121, Sonoma, CA 95476
cornerstonegardens.com
Visit year-round; art gardens are prettiest in the spring

📞 (707) 933-3010
🕐 Open daily 10am–4pm
$ Admission free
🐕 No dogs

Shimmering clouds of chicken wire and crystals float above cacti and crushed oyster shells in White Cloud, an art garden at Cornerstone Sonoma.

Gardens, wine, and shopping—it may sound like the title of a Strauss waltz, but it's what Cornerstone Sonoma is all about. This unique combination of outdoor market and art gardens in the heart of California's Wine Country lets you explore some interesting gardens, sip a glass of wine, and squeeze in some upscale shopping—all in one pleasant location. There's food, too, of course, and sometimes there's live music. Better give yourself a couple of hours to enjoy it all. And bring a sun hat.

Cornerstone Sonoma is located on the east side of Highway 121, about forty-four miles north of San Francisco. It has a lot to catch your eye and pique your senses. But it's the assemblage of small gardens designed by an international roster of landscape architects and designers that gives Cornerstone its garden edge.

The idea for an outdoor gallery of contemporary gardens started well over a decade ago when Chris Hougie and Teresa Raffo visited the International Garden Festival at Chaumont-sur-Loire in France. At this yearly event, about thirty landscape artists create gardens on a specific theme that typically involves the interaction of art, architecture, and nature. When the California couple inaugurated Cornerstone (then called Cornerstone Festival of Gardens), the invited artists didn't have to adhere to a theme. They were each given 1,800 square feet of land on which to create their gardens, art installations, or landscape statements. Until 2016, there were twenty side-by-side gardens in this one-of-a-kind garden gallery. Today there are nine.

The change occurred when the property was sold, the new owner re-envisioned the space, and *Sunset* magazine came into the picture. A premier West Coast lifestyle magazine, *Sunset* needed a place for new test gardens and an outdoor demonstration kitchen. It was a perfect fit for Cornerstone, but it meant that over half of the art gardens had to be removed to make room. Luckily, the nine remaining gardens were the most edgy, interesting, and playful of the original group. And the presence of *Sunset* brings a contemporary, homegrown relevance to Cornerstone by promoting and demonstrating how to grow and enjoy your own fruits, flowers, and vegetables.

The five new *Sunset* test gardens and outdoor kitchen take up about a quarter of an acre along the south edge of the property. Designed by Homestead Design Collective, the gardens are themed rooms devoted to interesting ornamental plants that can also be harvested and used in entertaining. The Cocktail Garden features lemon and other citrus trees, pomegranates, pineapple, guava, and hops, all used to augment, infuse, or flavor drinks. The Backyard Orchard focuses on stone fruit trees underplanted with ornamental grasses and perennials. In the Farm Garden, veggies are grown in raised beds and cherry tomatoes are trained on stainless steel trellises. The Flower Room showcases unusual flowers and shrubs, while the Gathering Space highlights the retail plant line offered by *Sunset*. The outdoor kitchen is used for creating, testing, demonstrating, and photographing new recipes and kitchen crafts.

The art garden installations are located just beyond the *Sunset* gardens and range along the eastern perimeter of the complex. The first one you'll see is John Greenlee's *Mediterranean Meadow*. Greenlee is a leading expert on ornamental grasses and sedges, and that's what he's planted on this prairielike hillock. Walk through on the winding path. It's a lovely, simple garden, full of movement and subtle colors that shift with the changing light of day. Taiwan-born landscape designer Conway Cheng Chang's *In the Air* is an installation that uses plants to ask questions about plant and human interdependence and adaptability to air. Next to it is *Garden of Contrast*, a beautiful work by James A. van Sweden and Sheila Brady. Here, a circular space divided into small fields by a rosemary hedge is planted with low grasses, agaves, and bright poppies. Beyond it is *Eucalyptus Soliloquy* by Walter Hood and Alma Du Solier, a corridor of walls created from Sonoma's nonnative eucalyptus trees, which form a windbreak between the fields and the surrounding vineyard. The naturally decaying eucalyptus wood, leaves, and seeds are an integral part of the installation.

California is an agricultural giant that depends upon thousands of migrant workers to harvest its crops. *Small Tribute to Immigrant Workers*, created by Mario Schjetnan of Mexico City, is a strong, simple memorial with portraits of farmworkers and a small shrine set into a stone wall above a reflecting pool. Roger

The Garden of Visceral Serenity, Yoji Sasaki's peaceful contribution at Cornerstone Sonoma, is surrounded by shrubbery.

Raiche and David McCrory of Planet Horticulture in San Francisco created *Rise*, the installation beside it. The piece consists of a hill planted with trees and shrubs, with a large corrugated metal pipe passing through it. When you walk through the pipe you enter a different garden space on the other side.

The Garden of Visceral Serenity by Yoji Sasaki of Osaka, Japan, is a quietly reflective enclosed garden. A granite stone path runs through it, with diagonal side ribs forming a calm white pattern in the low-growing grass. To one side is a meditation box made of rusted metal. *White Cloud*, the piece next to it, couldn't be more different. This work by landscape artists Andy Cao of Los Angeles and Xavier Perrot of Paris is like a whimsical illustration by Dr. Seuss—clouds of chicken wire and crystals float above an undulating landscape of crushed oyster shells inset with cacti.

Finally, there's the Sonoma Children's Garden by MIG of Berkeley. This garden is on a kid's level, planted with a simple, sturdy maze of vines, with paths for running and exploring, while a bevy of colorful birdhouses keep watch. In fact, all the gardens at Cornerstone are kid-friendly, although the intellectual content of some will be lost on youngsters.

And now's a good time for that glass of wine.

ferrari-carano
vineyards and winery

Small but lush garden within a winery
in the picturesque Sonoma countryside

8761 Dry Creek Road, Healdsburg, CA 95448
ferrari-carano.com
Visit March and April for tulip display

....

- 📞 (707) 433-6700 or (800) 831-0381
- 🕐 Open daily 10am–5pm, except major holidays
- 💲 Admission free; fee for wine tastings
- 🐕 No dogs

If you're visiting the wine country north of San Francisco and would like to combine a wine tasting with a garden visit, Ferrari-Carano Vineyards and Winery makes for a pleasant stop. The gardens here are not extensive, but they're pretty, peaceful, and impeccably maintained.

There's more than a little Las Vegas extravagance at play in this hugely successful winery. Not surprising, since the owners, Don and Rhonda Carano, made their mark with a hotel and casino in Reno, Nevada. Anyone who knows anything about having a successful hotel knows that attention to detail is everything. You'll see that here, in the immaculately groomed grounds, vineyards, gardens, and the enormous Tuscan-style Villa Fiore that serves as the tasting room, *enoteca*, and retail center.

The Caranos never planned to create a California wine empire, but they're the kind of people who don't do anything in a half-hearted manner. They first visited Sonoma County in the late 1970s on a wine-buying trip for their hotel. The intoxicating beauty of the Northern California wine country, where grapes have been grown since the 1850s, took hold of them almost immediately. They fell in love with the countryside because it reminded them of Tuscany, and a year later they purchased their first seventy acres of *terroir*. Today they have four vineyards in addition to this one in Dry Creek Valley, five appellations in all (an appellation is a legal designation of an area for growing wine grapes).

The five-acre walled garden Rhonda created in the old prune orchard is meant to complement Villa Fiore and the surrounding vineyards. It's really a pleasure garden, a place to stroll and relax among some 2,000 species of plants. This is not a mature, long-established garden—it was planted in the space of eight months—but you will find mature plants within it. Something is blooming or of seasonal interest year-round.

Villa Fiore, with its tasting room and lovely outdoor terrace, overlooks the Ferrari-Carano vineyards.

Before you enter the garden, I feel obliged to send out a *Tulipa* alert. If you suffer from tulipomania, and like to feast your eyes on vast displays of tulips and daffodils to get your gardening motor running in the spring, plan your visit to Ferrari-Carano for March. That's when there's a no-holds-barred floor show featuring 10,000 tulips and daffodils arranged in beds and around a spouting fountain in front of the villa. It's a sight that would make all those old Tuscan winemakers drop their jaws in wonder. All this and good wine, too? Let's call it Appellation Spring. If you miss the tulips and visit later in the year, you'll find other showy performers in their place. Giant begonias, perhaps.

A gate laden with wisteria and framed by hornbeams welcomes you to the grounds of this wine estate. A long, curved pathway leads up a gentle incline lined with a lush, manicured lawn to Villa Fiore. This was formerly flatland, like the vineyards that surround the villa. About halfway up you'll pass a giant bronze sculpture of a wild boar. Beyond that is the entrance to the villa, with a sunny terrace in front overlooking the vineyards and the fountain garden. Stop in here if you want to do a wine tasting or sample their signature fume blanc.

The walled garden, called the Arena, is down and to the side of the villa. In the hot, dry Sonoma summers, the garden with its trees and water-feature stream is the coolest spot on the property. A bevy of specimen trees provides much of the interest. Upon entering, you'll encounter a weeping Norway spruce (*Picea abies* 'Pendula') and beautiful river birches (*Betula nigra*). Spring blossoms adorn ornamental trees like the Japanese snowbell tree (*Styrax japonicus*); *Camellia japonica* 'Nuccio's Pearl', with vivid, roselike flowers; a Kousa dogwood; and a tulip tree (*Liriodendron tulipifera*) or saucer magnolia (*Magnolia ×soulangeana*). And since you're at a winery, have a look at the three cork trees (*Quercus suber*). This species is the principle source of cork for wine bottles.

A stream threads through the garden between ponds at either end. A small Japanese-style garden around the far pond is planted with Japanese flowering cherries (*Prunus* 'Kanzan') with double white blossoms in the spring, weeping Japanese cherries (*Prunus subhirtella* 'Pendula') with pink blossoms, and Japanese maples (*Acer palmatum* 'Seiryu') that turn crimson in the fall.

Hundreds of specimen plants are found at Ferrari-Carano Vineyards and Winery, among them *Quercus suber* (cork oak), the tree used for making wine corks.

When your garden visit is over, head back to Villa Fiore to enjoy a glass of *vino* on that sunny terrace. From there, the expansive view of neatly tended vineyards and silvery green olive trees might trick you into thinking you really are in Tuscany.

quarryhill botanical garden

12841 Sonoma Highway, Glen Ellen, CA 95442
quarryhillbg.org
Visit year-round; April–June for maximum blooms

- 📞 (707) 996-3166
- 🕐 Open daily 9am–4pm (entrance closes at 3pm); closed major holidays
- $ Admission fee
- ♿ Hilly terrain and gravel pathways may be unsuitable for wheelchairs
- 🐕 No dogs

Secluded haven devoted to Asian plants grown from wild-collected seeds

Some gems are hidden but shouldn't be. Quarryhill is a truly great botanical garden, yet many people drive past and have no inkling of the riches to be found beyond the grape vines seen from the road. Head to the visitor center, though, and embark on a unique, informative, and enchanting garden experience.

Quarryhill is better known internationally than nationally, in part because of its close partnership with the Royal Botanic Gardens at Kew, in England. Jane Davenport Jansen, who bought the 62-acre property in 1968, wanted her garden to focus on plants from Asia and to be dedicated to conservation. That meant all plants had to come from seeds collected in the wild, and records had to be kept of their provenance and growth habits once planted. Before any plantings got underway, Jansen and her garden designer consulted with the botanists at Kew and the UC Botanical Garden at Berkeley. The goal was not to create an ornamental garden, but a garden that looked completely natural. Each plant in the extraordinary palette was planted in what was considered its best location. There are no formal groupings, no imposed style, yet everything looks completely at home.

And yes, every plant, shrub, and tree was grown from seed collected in the wild on plant expeditions to China, the Himalayas, Japan, and Korea. This garden is all the more remarkable when you consider that planting didn't begin until 1987, making Quarryhill one of California's newest—yet oldest-feeling—botanical gardens. The garden is beautiful year-round, but really shines in the spring and early summer, when the surrounding foothills of the Mayacamas Mountains are green and many of the exotic trees and shrubs are in full flower.

Strolling through this lush garden, it's hard to imagine what it looked like when Jansen bought the property. Back then, the entire area was recovering from a massive wildfire that had swept through the mountains in 1964. Thickets of fast-growing madrone and knobcone pine had re-established themselves on the hillsides but little else grew. A rock quarry operation had gouged out deep declivities in the valley floor, where a stream once flowed. Today those old eyesore quarries are Monet-like ponds shimmering with pink and white waterlilies, and the once charred hillsides

A stone lion, symbol of prosperity and longevity, stands guard at Quarryhill Botanical Garden in Sonoma.

are covered with thousands of plants that are rare, threatened, or endangered in their native habitats.

On your way to the wild portion of the garden, you'll pass a circular rose garden overlooked by a spectacular yellow Lady Banks' rose that has made its home in a giant oak. This garden tells the story of the Chinese origins of the modern rose. In a nutshell, about half of the 200 or so wild roses in the world are found in China; their predominant trait is that they are repeaters (they bloom more than once during the growing season). The old roses of Europe, on the other hand, had a single bloom in the spring. About two centuries ago, the tea rose and the China rose made their way from China to Europe and were crossed with European varieties. Four new roses, the so-called stud roses, were created and became the progenitors of all modern hybrid roses. Four quadrants in the rose garden are planted with examples of these studs, which look rather delicate and demure.

Farther on, two stone pillars mark the entrance to Quarryhill's real glory: the 25-acre botanical garden. Wide gravel paths meander up and down hillsides planted with wild (and wild-collected) rhododendrons, camellias, peonies, and magnolias, among others. A map from the visitor center pinpoints some of the rarer specimens, and plants are labeled. If you take the path that heads south from the entrance pillars, you'll come to a rare and critically threatened Chinese maple (*Acer pentaphyllum*) that grows only along the Yalong River in western Sichuan. Plans are underway to dam the Yalong, which will submerge and destroy this tree's entire native habitat. It's an example of why these plants are disappearing in the wild, and why it's so important to conserve them in places like Quarryhill.

At the north end of the nearby semicircular arbor path, *Rosa chinensis* var. *spontanea*, a China rose once thought to be extinct, cascades over a rock wall and blossoms with pink, white, or red flowers in February or March. From here, take the path heading east to see *Cornus capitata*, a lovely evergreen dogwood from southern Sichuan that was a favorite of Jane Jansen.

Speaking of trees, look for the rare *Emmenopterys henryi*, which grows beside a path in the very heart of the garden. Renowned English plant explorer Ernest Wilson pronounced it "one of the most strikingly beautiful trees in the Chinese forest." He took specimens back to England, where they stubbornly refused to blossom for seventy-five years—though the specimen

at Quarryhill flowered after just six. The garden is also home to a dawn redwood (*Metasequoia glyptostroboides*), a deciduous Chinese redwood closely related to coast and Sierra redwoods and long thought to be extinct in the wild. In 1941, a stand was discovered in a remote valley in central China. If you're visiting in winter, you'll also be dazzled by the thick red-orange berry clusters on the dioecious ligiri tree (*Idesia polycarpa*) from Japan.

As for color, the orange-red to salmon-red blossoms of the Japanese azalea (*Rhododendron japonicum*) delight the eye every spring. And for fragrance, the early autumn leaves of the Katsura tree (*Cercidiphyllum japonicum*) produce a scent that smells like cotton candy to some, fresh strawberries to others.

Take your time at Quarryhill and you'll leave with a deeper appreciation of the richness of Asia's native flora, as well as an increased awareness of the environmental pressures that threaten wild plants everywhere.

Splashy blooms bring color to the Carmel Mission, established in Carmel-by-the-Sea in 1771 by Father Junípero Serra.

central &
north coast

mendocino coast botanical gardens

18220 North Highway 1, Fort Bragg, CA 95437
gardenbythesea.org
Visit year-round; February–May for rhododendrons and
    camellias; May–July for wildflowers, roses, succulents,
    begonias; August for heathers

....

- 📞 (707) 964-4352
- 🕐 Open daily 9am–5pm (Nov–Mar until 4pm); closed
    Thanksgiving, Dec 25
- $ Admission fee
- 🐕 Dogs on leash

Mendocino Coast
Botanical Gardens
are unique in their
ocean frontage.

Oceanside setting with cliffside walks, native plants, and heritage plant collections

The Mendocino Coast Botanical Gardens, among the few botanical gardens in the continental United States located right on the ocean, are worth visiting just for the spectacular clifftop walks high above the surging waves. But it so happens that these forty-seven acres of oceanside nirvana are also home to a significant botanical garden, with notable collections of rhododendrons, camellias, heirloom roses, heathers, native plants, and so much more. You should give yourself at least two hours to enjoy all it has to offer. If it's a beautiful day, bring a picnic lunch (or have lunch at the seasonal Rhody's Garden Café) and stay longer.

The garden is located in Fort Bragg, about 170 miles (three and a half hours) northwest of San Francisco. The most scenic route from the city is Highway 101 to Cloverdale, and Highway 128 to Albion; you'll pass through an area of towering redwoods on the way. If you want to make this an overnight trip, Mendocino, about seven miles south of the garden, is a charming town full of bed-and-breakfast options and Victorian-era inns. The coast here is not immune to winter storms and rains, but it's generally mild and benign; coastal fog can be thick, especially in summer. The best time to visit the gardens is February through May, when the rhododendrons and camellias are in bloom, but something is blooming every month of the year.

In the early 1960s, a retired nurseryman named Ernie Schoefer bought the land, loaded it up with ornamental flowers, and put up a sign to lure tourists from Highway 101 into Flowerland by the Sea. Ernie provided a place where the area's newly formed garden clubs could grow experimental plantings to test for hardiness; those plantings were the genesis for the botanical garden.

It was something of a struggle, though, to make this the botanical haven it is today. Ernie's son sold Flowerland to developers in the early 1970s and they, of course, wanted to build on the land. The community and Mendocino County worked together to save the plants and the property's public access to the coast. The Coastal Conservancy bought the twelve acres closest to Highway 101, where the historic plant collections are located. About ten years later they purchased the additional thirty-five acres of ocean-front. The property was then turned over to Mendocino Parks and Recreation, and a nonprofit was formed to administer the newly formed botanical garden.

Steps lead down from the entrance plaza to the various collections. Native Bishop pines (*Pinus muricata*), the signature pine of this coastal area, have been planted as a windbreak along the garden's southern boundary. You come first to the colorful Perennial Garden, planted in irregularly shaped island beds. From spring through fall, this seasonal showstopper is filled with bright, bold colors and unusual foliage combinations. To the west is the delightfully old-fashioned Heritage Rose Garden, in bloom from May through September. Every rose you see was discovered along the roadside or growing on old homesteads and ranches in Mendocino County. The plants were collected by two sisters who scoured the countryside throughout Northern California to find and preserve old heirloom roses planted by nineteenth-century pioneers.

In summer, don't miss the floral extravaganza in the Mae E. Lauer Display House. The entire house is given over to masses of pink, red, purple, lavender, and white fuchsia standards growing in pots below brilliant baskets of tuberous begonias. Butterflies flit through and hummingbirds dart in for a sip of nectar.

Just to the north, you'll find the impressive Heath and Heather Collection, recognized by the American Public Gardens Association as a collection of national significance. Mendocino's mild maritime climate and sandy acidic soil is ideal for these sun-loving plants, which provide subtle jewel tones of color into late summer and foliage colors ranging from copper, pink, gold, and silvery gray to almost every shade of green.

The garden is best known for its Rhododendron Collection garden, the largest such collection in California, with about 1,000 plants (125 species, 190 cultivars) blooming from November through July. The plants are so beloved that a "Rhododendrons Blooming" sign is displayed when the flowers peak in April and May. It's the botanical equivalent of whale watching. This important collection was augmented in 1994 by a large bequest of tender species rhododendrons from the mountainous regions of Burma, China, and Tibet, and big-leaf rhododendrons with leaf sizes up to 25 inches long. Unlike the rhodie hybrids we're used to, the tender species rhododendrons have an intoxicating fragrance.

More plant collections are found on the north side of the garden, including succulents, camellias, dahlias, and a Mediterranean Garden with plants from the five Mediterranean regions of the world. But what makes this botanical garden truly unique is its oceanside location. It's really three gardens in one: a heritage plant collection area, a transitional woodland zone with native plants, and a sweep of maritime prairie headland.

To reach the ocean, you'll pass through The Narrows—the old public right-of-way that the Coast Conservancy fought to keep public. The path along Fern Creek is a living encyclopedia of the native plants that thrive in damp coastal forests here and throughout the Pacific Northwest (the so-called Vancouverian floristic province): wild ginger, red alder, Oregon grape (*Mahonia*), bleeding heart (*Dicentra*), red elderberry, salmonberry, false Solomon's seal, honeysuckle, and 165 species of fungi. Look for swamp bellflower (*Campanula californica*), a lovely wildflower that grows only along the coast between Marin and Mendocino counties. A new bridge erected over once-dammed Fern Creek allows steelhead to spawn again.

When you leave the woods, a stretch of high maritime prairie opens out in front of you. It's a dramatic and exciting transition from the cultivated gardens and sheltered woodland to waves roaring in to crash along a rocky shore. This area, once grazed, is now being replanted with native wildflowers. From the headland you might spot migrating gray whales or, closer to shore, sinuous brown forests of bull kelp shimmering in the surging Pacific waters. The bull kelp is a plant, too—part of the diverse flora in this fascinating botanical garden.

The extensive Heath and Heather Collection is just one of the many specialty gardens at Mendocino Coast Botanical Gardens.

the secret gardens of monterey

Charming public gardens
tucked amid historic sites in
the heart of old Monterey

A flowery corner near
the Joseph Boston
& Co. store, one of
Monterey's oldest
adobe buildings.

Various locations in downtown Monterey, all within a half-mile of each other
parks.ca.gov; historicgardenleague.org
Visit year-round; March–May for maximum blooms

··

- 📞 (831) 649-7118 (California Parks); (831) 649-3364 (Historic Garden League)
- 🕐 Gardens open daily 9am–4pm (summer until 5pm); open times for historic buildings varies by day and season
- $ Admission free
- ♿ Some of the gardens have stairs and pathways not suitable for wheelchairs
- 🐕 No dogs

Most visitors to Monterey put the Monterey Bay Aquarium at the top of their must-see list. Not me. It's Monterey's secret gardens that I head to first. Of course you should visit the aquarium, too—among the world's most acclaimed. But if you're a garden lover and a history or architecture buff, you'll be delightfully surprised to discover the heritage urban gardens tucked away in the heart of old Monterey. On a leisurely two-hour self-guided walking tour, you can visit several of these charming garden nooks *and* see some of the oldest buildings in California. Touring the gardens will give you an intimate glimpse of historic Monterey that many tourists never see. I love to stay at the Monterey Hotel (montereyhotel.com) in the heart of downtown. It dates from 1904 but has been completely updated, and all the gardens are close by.

Though parts of Monterey look new and mall-like today, it is actually one of the oldest cities in California. It served as the Spanish and then Mexican capital of Alta California from 1770 until 1846. It was also home to an enormous fishing industry (immortalized by John Steinbeck in his 1945 novel, *Cannery Row*) that collapsed in the 1950s due to overfishing. The buildings you'll see on this tour date from the mid-nineteenth century, but the gardens created around them are from the 1920s and later. Six of the gardens are owned by the state of California and administered as the Monterey State Historic Park. However, it's thanks to the tireless volunteer efforts of the nonprofit Historic Garden League that the secret gardens of Monterey are maintained, preserved, and interpreted.

Docent-led tours can be arranged April–September through the Historic Garden League. But if you're on your own, start at the fragrant Casa del Oro Herb Garden near the corner of Scott and Olivier Streets. To one side is the Picket Fence (open Fri–Sat 11am–3pm), headquarters of the Historic Garden League, where you can pick up a walking-tour map of the gardens. Their store and gallery is located in the adjacent Joseph Boston & Co. store (open Thurs–Sun 11am–3pm), a two-story adobe building erected in 1848 during the Gold Rush era. It got its nickname, Casa del Oro (House of Gold), from the prospectors who stashed their glittering nuggets in the store's safe, the first one in Northern California (it's still there). The old-fashioned garden outside the store is planted with a variety of herbs, including lavender, oregano, thyme, rosemary, sorrel, and purple and white sage. Orange blossom perfumes the air in the spring and a beautiful old Cécile Brünner rose climbs up the adobe wall.

Cross the plant-filled pedestrian walkway in front of the Picket Fence and step into the courtyard of the lovely Memory Garden at Pacific House, a two-story Spanish-style structure built in 1847 for Thomas Oliver Larkin. A Massachusetts-born merchant, Larkin served as the first (and last) U.S. Consul to Mexican California and then helped to usher California into U.S. statehood. The building, which now houses a local-history museum, was rented out for use as an army barracks, a warehouse, a tavern, and the first county courthouse. Before it became a garden, the patio area was a corral and the site of vicious bear-and-bull fights, a favorite spectator sport of the time. The building was later purchased by the same man who bought the Joseph Boston & Co. store across the way. In 1927, Larkin's daughters added the arcaded courtyard and hired none other than Frederick Law Olmsted, Jr., son of the man who created New York's Central Park, to design a romantic version of an Andalusian-style garden. It's a lovely spot, with evergreen magnolias shading a central fountain, Belle Portugaise roses dangling in clusters above the arched stucco walls, and citrus and jasmine spicing the air. Pink camellias, purple snowball bushes, hydrangeas, fuchsias, pomegranates and an Australian tea tree also survive from the 1920s.

Now head over to the nearby Custom House overlooking Monterey Bay. This long adobe building is the oldest government building in California and the first designated California Historic Landmark. It was used by the Mexican government from 1822 to

The Memory Garden, designed by Frederick Law Olmsted, Jr., graces the courtyard of Monterey's Pacific House.

1846 and taken over by the United States in 1848 when California was annexed. During the Spanish-Mexican period, Monterey was the port of entry for all goods arriving in California, and it was here that cargo was examined and taxed. The dry, dusty garden at the far side of the Custom House is devoted to desert plants, many of them cacti native to Mexico and the U.S. Southwest, as well as bromeliads, tree aloes, a ponytail palm, and a dragon tree. Replanted after being excavated for building upgrades in the 1990s, it's not the most interesting or well-maintained garden in Monterey, but it does let you see the variety of succulents that can grow in Monterey's Mediterranean climate.

Next stop is the 1847 adobe-and-frame Old Whaling Station, bounded by Scott, Olivier, and Pacific Streets. Have a look at the black-and-white paving tiles made from whale bones. In 1855 the Old Monterey Whaling Company began using the site for its onshore whaling operations, reducing blubber to lamp oil in the huge iron cauldron in the rear garden. The building was eventually restored and a Victorian-style courtyard garden was laid out between the Old Whaling Station and the first brick building in California. The garden features heirloom roses, boxwood and privet hedges, and loquat, pepper, and Catalina cherry trees planted around brick walkways.

The Doud House Garden, at the corner of Scott and Van Buren Streets, is a romantic little residential garden created around a house built in the 1850s. The four Monterey cypress trees on the property were planted by the original owners. In the 1960s, landscape architect Florence Yoch redesigned the grounds for a friend who had bought the historic property. Yoch, whose career in Hollywood included designing the garden sets for *Gone with the Wind* (she also helped design the beautiful gardens at Rancho Los Alamitos) created a quiet, charming, period-appropriate garden. Here, a climbing Belle Portugaise rose and a Chinese wisteria intertwine on a small pergola, and agapanthus, a Catalina ironwood, an oakleaf hydrangea, white hellebores, and salvias are planted around the house and its little front porch. By the 1980s, the garden had become overgrown. It's being reclaimed and maintained by the ever-busy volunteers of the Historic Garden League.

Huge Monterey cypresses grow around the garden at California's First Theatre on the corner of Pacific and Scott Streets. Yes, this small frame structure (not open to the public) was really the first theater in California. It was built in 1846–47 by a British adventurer named Jack Swan, who originally used it as a lodging house and bar. A couple of years later he began staging theatrical performances (men played all the roles, including the female ones, just as in Shakespeare's day). An enormous chalice vine (*Solandra*

The garden behind Casa Soberanes is considered to be the oldest continuously used garden in Monterey.

maxima) laden with golden cups of yellow blossoms covers one end of the building. Besides the venerable Monterey cypresses, the garden area around the old theater contains a pink-blossomed magnolia tree, an avocado, a buddleia, and a giant sequoia (*Sequoiadendron giganteum*), one of the three redwood species that are symbols of California.

Blue gates in a chalk rock wall open into the front and back gardens of Casa Soberanes, an impressive two-story Mexican Colonial–style adobe house (known locally as the House of the Blue Gate) at the corner of Pacific and Del Monte. It was built in 1842, when Monterey was still under Mexican rule; the Soberanes family lived here from 1860 until 1922 (the last Soberanes to inherit the property was a gardener at the Carmel Mission). This is considered the oldest continuously used garden in Monterey, with a pepper tree and a grape vine in back that can be traced back to the late nineteenth century. The semi-formal, cottage-style garden design you see today dates from the 1920s. The terraced grounds, surrounded by a cypress hedge, are planted with fragrant Mexican orange blossom (*Choisya ternata*), colorful Spanish bluebells (*Hyacinthoides hispanica*), an apricot tree, and an assortment of flowering perennials. The flower beds, as you'll see elsewhere in Monterey, are neatly edged with upended wine bottles, abalone shells, even whale bones, all of which have their own stories to tell about old Monterey.

From Monterey you can easily explore the rest of the Monterey Peninsula by taking the famous 17-Mile Drive from Pacific Grove to Carmel-by-the-Sea. Pacific Grove, about 2.5 miles north of Monterey, is where the monarch butterflies overwinter in the pine and eucalyptus trees (Monarch Grove Butterfly Sanctuary) on their annual migration to and from Mexico. The drive winds along a spectacular section of central California coastline, now a protected marine sanctuary, where distinctive Monterey pines and Monterey cypresses are the predominant native trees. At artsy Carmel-by-the-Sea you can visit Carmel Mission, founded in 1771 by Father Junipero Serra. The Franciscan friars under Father Serra introduced the concept of agricultural gardening to the area's tribes, forcing many Native Americans to work as field laborers. Father Serra was canonized by Pope Francis in 2015, but his elevation to sainthood was controversial, to say the least. The pretty gardens around the Carmel Mission were added during twentieth-century restoration work.

university of california santa cruz arboretum

Largest collection of Australian plants outside Australia, plus sections devoted to South Africa, New Zealand, and California

1156 High Street, Santa Cruz, CA 95064
arboretum.ucsc.edu
Visit March–May for maximum color and bloom

The UC Santa Cruz Arboretum has more plants from Australia than any botanical garden outside Australia.

- 📞 (831) 502-2998
- 🕐 Open daily 9am–5pm; closed Thanksgiving, Dec 25
- $ Admission fee, includes docent-led tour; free tour on first Saturday of the month
- 🐕 No dogs

You may be wondering if you just wandered into a corner of Australia. You have. It just happens to be on the campus of the University of California, Santa Cruz (UC Santa Cruz). This 135-acre arboretum has the largest collection of plants from Down Under outside of . . . well, Down Under.

And talk about a grassroots organization. The story behind the creation and maintenance of this fascinating arboretum is a testament to the dedication and determination of plant lovers inside and outside the groves of academe. It's not the most aesthetically arresting garden you'll ever visit. The emphasis is on the plants rather than the landscaping. But it's a wonderful place to wander

for an hour or two, preferably in the spring or early summer when trees and shrubs are in bright, vibrant bloom and hummingbirds, bees, and butterflies are plentiful.

Though it has always been affiliated with the university, the arboretum originated and got its first plants in 1965, four years before the Santa Cruz campus opened. The site, overlooking Monterey Bay, with a deep ravine and three tributaries of Moore Creek running through it, was handpicked by Dean McHenry, the founding chancellor. The great nature photographer Ansel Adams was also influential in preserving and protecting the site from commercial development.

The first plants? Eucalyptus trees from Australia. The arboretum now has fifty species of eucalyptus, more than any other arboretum in the country, and the Eucaplytus Grove stands at the southern end of the property. In 1967 deodar cedars were added, the first conifers to be planted in the arboretum. Today the conifer collection contains representatives of all but four of the world's known genera, some extremely rare. Except for the California natives, all the specimens that were eventually collected and planted are from the Southern Hemisphere (Australia, South

Africa, New Zealand), places with Mediterranean climates similar to that of coastal California.

Despite the fact that it's affiliated with UC Santa Cruz, university funding for the arboretum has always been erratic and precarious. In 1994, university support shriveled to almost nothing. As a result, the arboretum has had to broaden its appeal to the general public and scramble to support its ongoing research mission. Without the generosity of individual donors, ongoing grants, and help from hundreds of volunteers, this important repository of rare and endangered plants would not be able to survive. Buildings, roads, pathways, plantings, upkeep—they're all the result of volunteer labor.

Before exploring more exotic botanical treasures, have a good sniff around the Aroma Garden near the entrance and admire the Succulent Garden planted just north of it. The collection of *Dudleya* species is the largest in the world. With basal rosettes of thick gray to green leaves, these drought-tolerant succulents from the hot, dry U.S. Southwest are often inconspicuous until they send up their eye-catching flower stalks.

The South Africa section at UC Santa Cruz Arboretum is reminiscent of that country's fynbos shrubland.

Wander at will or follow a couple of self-guided trails. For an overview of the entire arboretum, take the 1.75-mile World Tour Trail. If you're here in March, with the hummingbirds, you'll enjoy the short, quarter-mile Hummingbird Trail that takes you to an outstanding location for viewing Anna's hummingbirds.

The Australian Garden takes up the northern half of the grounds and is the largest of the arboretum's four geographical sections. The most important collection here is called the Banksia Field. *Banksia*, a genus of the family Proteaceae, is endemic to coastal Australia, where many species are now rare and endangered. Plants range in size from low-growing shrubs to trees. The showy flower spikes, often yellow or red, ooze nectar—that's why hummingbirds, bees, bats, and other nectarivorous animals love them. Later, they send up fruiting "cones" that look like Christmas candles.

Just to the east of the Banksia Field is the arboretum's newest (and still unfinished) planting area, the Australian Rock Garden. A dense grove of redwoods serves as a boundary at the north end of the property. The beds of ericaceous plants in the five-acre South Africa Garden were some of the arboretum's earliest plantings; these low-growing heaths and heathers turn into brilliant mounds of color when they flower in the spring and fall. They share the South Africa Garden with one of the world's finest collections of South African proteas, including leucadendrons and leucospermums. Leucadendrons are typically smallish evergreen shrubs with simple elliptical leaves, but some of them can grow into trees—the endangered silvertree (*Leucadendron argenteum*), with its gray bark and silvery white leaves, is one striking example. *Leucospermum* species, commonly known as pincushion proteas because their flowerheads look as though they're stuck full of needles, are also shrubby, evergreen members of the family Proteaceae. In the wild, all these plants grow in a landscape called the *fynbos*, a scrubby, shrubby heathland on the Western Cape of South Africa.

Primitive flowering plants (angiosperms) and South Pacific conifers were the first plants collected for the New Zealand Garden and form the core of the collection. Plant historians take note: this arboretum is the only place in the world that cultivates *Amborella trichopoda*. According to DNA analysis, this primitive angiosperm from the shady forests of New Caledonia is among the oldest flowering plants in the world—a direct descendant of the forerunner of all flowering plants in the world.

You'll find more familiar plants in the two areas set aside for California natives. The Natives Come First Garden is a kind of introductory display to promote interest in California flora. A much larger, 50-acre section on Lower Moore Creek is called the California Province Garden. The specimen plants you'll find in these sections were collected from Santa Cruz Island, the Central and South Coast Ranges, and the North Coast and Klamath Ranges. A special feature is the native bulb garden, which includes calochortus, triteleias, and fritillaries.

Before you leave, stop in and have a look at the plants and gardening goods at Norrie's Gift and Garden Shop near the entrance. You might find a special piece of Down Under to take home with you.

Santa Barbara

Santa Barbara Channel

Santa Cruz
Island

Ventura

San Gabriel
Mountains

Huntington Library, Art Collections,
and Botanical Gardens

Descanso
Gardens

Pasadena

Malibu

Los
Angeles

Los Angeles
County
Arboretum
and Botanic
Garden

Santa
Monica

Inglewood

Anaheim

Santa
Monica
Bay

South Coast
Botanic Garden

Long
Beach

Rancho
Los
Alamitos

Pacific
Ocean

California Scenario

Santa
Catalina
Island

Sherman Library
and Gardens

Hortense Miller
Garden

Santa Barbara Botanic Garden

Alice Keck Park Memorial Gardens

Hope
Ranch

**Santa
Barbara**

Lotusland

Montecito

**Casa del
Herrero**

Summerland

Stearn's
Wharf

Pacific
Ocean

Topanga

Santa Monica Mountains

Greystone
Mansion and
Gardens

**Virginia Robinson
Gardens**

West
Hollywood

Malibu

**Adamson
House**

PACIFIC

**Getty
Villa**

COAST

**Getty
Center**

Westwood

HIGHWAY

Santa
Monica

**Mildred E. Mathias
Botanical Garden**

Santa
Monica
Pier

Mar
Vista

Culver
City

Pacific
Ocean

southern
california

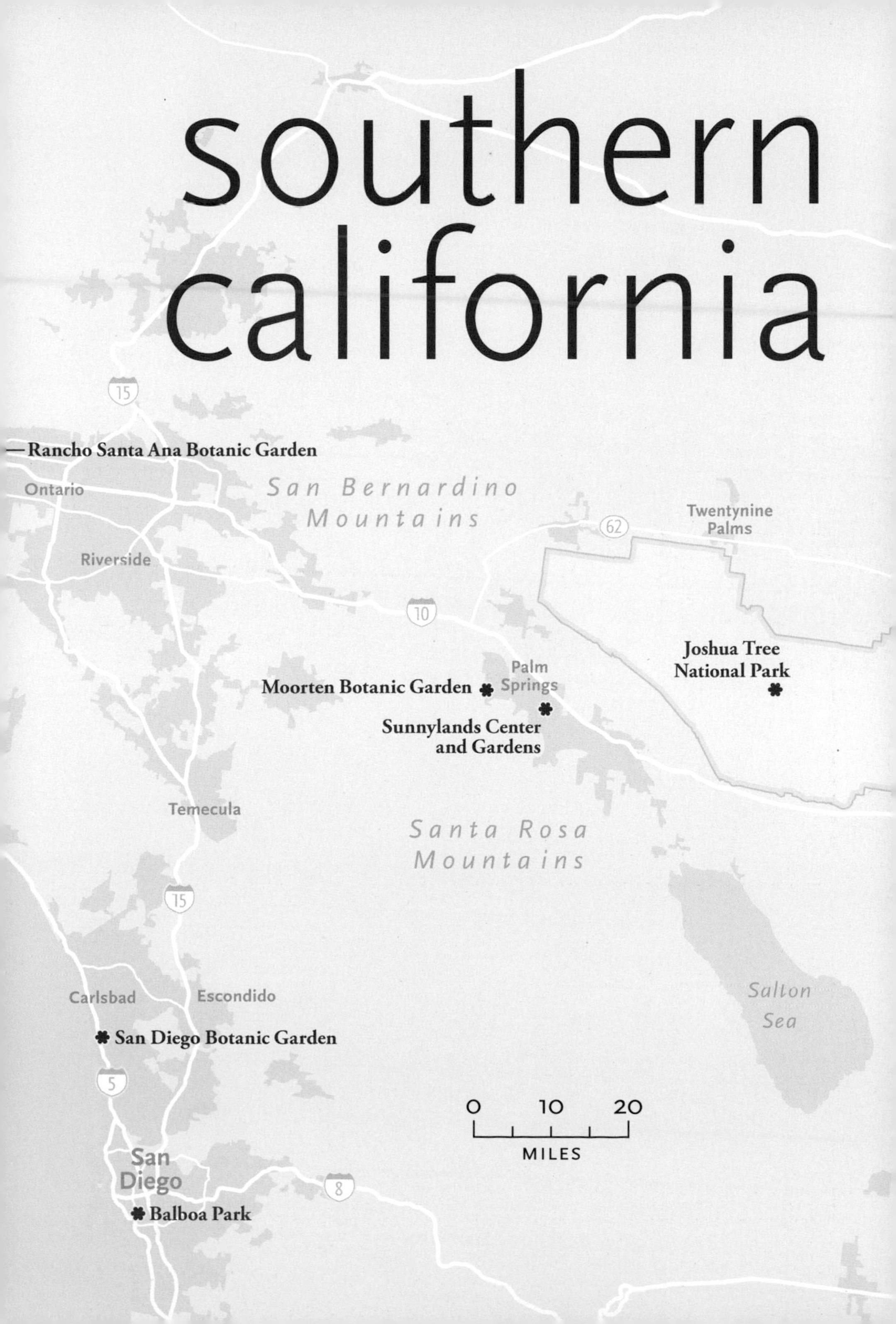

15

—Rancho Santa Ana Botanic Garden

Ontario

San Bernardino
Mountains

Twentynine
Palms

62

Riverside

10

Joshua Tree
National Park

Palm
Springs

Moorten Botanic Garden

Sunnylands Center
and Gardens

Temecula

Santa Rosa
Mountains

15

Carlsbad   Escondido

Salton
Sea

San Diego Botanic Garden

5

0   10   20

MILES

San
Diego

8

Balboa Park

los angeles & vicinity

Pink bougainvillea drapes a wall at the Getty Center in Los Angeles.

adamson house

23200 Pacific Coast Highway, Malibu, CA 90265
adamsonhouse.org
Visit year-round

....

- 📞 (310) 456-8432
- ⏰ Grounds open daily 8am–sunset; house and museum open Fri–Sat 11am–3pm
- $ Admission free for grounds; fee for house tour; no parking on grounds—paid parking in adjacent lot
- 🚌 Public transportation
- 🐕 No dogs

Breathtaking 1920s-era oceanside house and botanic garden in Malibu

Built with a view of Malibu Pier and the ocean, Rhoda and Merritt Huntley Adamson's beach cottage was decorated with tiles from Malibu Potteries.

Hidden behind nondescript stone walls along the Pacific Coast Highway just north of Malibu Pier is a magnificent oceanside estate. If you're interested in history, botany, or architecture, or all three, find a parking space in the adjacent city lot and make your way past the windmill palms that flank the entrance gate to the Adamson House. The grounds, with their eye-stretching views of Malibu Lagoon and Surfrider Beach, are a state park and open daily to the public (there's even a picnic table if you want to bring lunch). The house, a National Historic Site and California Historic Landmark, is open only on Fridays and Saturdays.

The thirteen acres that the Adamson house and gardens occupy today are only a tiny fraction of the 13,000 acres of Malibu beachfront property once owned by Frederick H. and Rhoda May Rindge. They bought the land in 1892, soon after Frederick inherited $2 million and they moved from Cambridge, Massachusetts, to California. Rindge then wrote a book called *Happy Days in Southern California*. If you owned all Malibu, you might be happy too. But there were fierce legal battles. Henry Huntington (of the Huntington Library, Art Collections, and Botanical Gardens) tried to extend his Southern Pacific Railroad right through the Rindges' property. Fred successfully thwarted Huntington's

plans by building his own railroad, but then the state of California wanted to build a road along the then-roadless coast. That, too, was challenged and rechallenged until finally the state and county took the land by eminent domain and constructed the Roosevelt Highway, now called the Pacific Coast Highway or Highway 1, which opened in 1928.

By that time, Fred was long dead and the enterprising Rhoda May had spent over twenty years building their Rancho Topanga Malibu Sequit into the most valuable real estate in the United States. She also started the acclaimed Malibu Potteries. The locally produced ceramic tiles with their Mediterranean-inspired designs were used in hundreds of homes throughout the West from 1926 until 1932.

When daughter Rhoda married Merritt Huntley Adamson, mother Rhoda May gifted them the beachside property known as Vaquero or Cowboy Hill. A new "beach cottage" surrounded by lush gardens and fountains went with it. Since the land was mostly sand dunes, it was necessary to truck in thousands of tons of topsoil. The Adamsons took possession of their new Hispano-Moorish beach house in 1929, and the younger Rhoda lived in it until 1962. The property was slated for redevelopment until concerned citizens rallied to save it. Eventually the state bought the property for use as a state park, but the house fell into disrepair and the neglected gardens became overgrown. Today, the restored house and gardens form a remarkable oceanside ensemble that typifies and illuminates a privileged Southern California lifestyle of the 1920s and 1930s.

DeWitt Norris, the landscape architect, worked with Morgan Evans (who would later do the landscaping at Disneyland) to create the multi-level gardens with their lush green lawns, vibrant flower beds, and collection of Mediterranean trees and shrubs. The gardens have been reduced over the years and don't look as bounteous as they did when six gardeners were on staff, but there is a lot here for garden lovers to enjoy, not least of which is the glinting blue backdrop of the Pacific.

The collection of mature palms and exotic flowering trees and shrubs is the most noteworthy feature of the gardens. On the lower tier, look for the Australian cow-itch trees (*Lagunaria patersonia*)—slender, broad-leaf evergreens with pink hibiscuslike flowers and nutlike seed capsules filled with irritating hairs. (Hence the itch, but why the cow?) On the lawn between the lath house (once used as a plant shed) and the gift shop, sniff out the gnarled but heavily perfumed tree gardenia (*Gardenia thunbergia*) from southeastern Africa. Several sorts of guava, including pineapple guava (*Acca sellowiana*) and lemon guava (*Psidium littorale*), planted in front of the tiny gift shop, are notable for their intensely colored flowers. "Flamboyant" is the only word to describe the long-blooming (up to eight months) marmalade bush (*Streptosolen jamesonii*) with its cascading clusters

of gold, peach, and orange flowers; look for it near the tilework fountain behind the house. Another flame-flowered beauty is the African coral tree or kaffirboom (*Erythrina caffra*), which is the official tree of Los Angeles; it grows on a slope above a patio on the landward side of the house. If the garden has one signature tree, it's the distinctive bunya-bunya (*Araucaria bidwillii*), an Australian native that looks like a pine (but isn't) and drops cones the size of bowling balls; it's one of the oldest tree species still in existence, dating back to the Cretaceous era. Scattered around the grounds you'll also find a lemon tree (*Citrus limonia*) from Burma, a pomegranate (*Punica granatum*) from Iran, and olive trees (*Olea europaea*) from Italy. Though it's not an exotic, the California sycamore (*Platanus racemosa*) that shades the Wedding Lawn near the entrance is spectacular in its girth and canopy.

Canary Island date palms (*Phoenix canariensis*), their fronds glistening in the sun and waving in the Pacific breezes, lend a tropical air to the property. Other palms in the collection include Senegal date palm (*P. reclinata*); an unusual multi-trunked Mediterranean fan palm (*Chamaerops humilis*); and California's only native palm, *Washingtonia robusta*.

The Adamson House is surrounded by a portion of the original gardens and can be visited on docent-led tours.

If you're not on a docent-led house tour, you'll have to content yourself with admiring the white stucco Adamson beach cottage from the outside. The front courtyard of flagstones set within bright green St. Augustine grass looks almost surreally at odds with the Spanish and Moorish-style architecture. The interior is fascinating because almost every room is decorated with ceramic tiles from Malibu Potteries; it is, in fact, the most complete assemblage of these tiles in the world. You can see them outside as well, on the wall fountains behind the house and in the rear patio, and on the Moorish-style, star-shaped fountain on the lower lawn. The former garage, which once berthed the Adamsons' three Pierce-Arrow automobiles, has been converted to the small Malibu Lagoon Museum of local history (open only when the house is open). Courtyards, patios, balconies, and service areas around the house are embellished with container plants, shaded by exotic trees, and festooned with colorful vines. There's also a swimming pool with a tile-embellished pavilion, a boat house and, of course, the whelping shed where the Adamsons' collies gave birth to more Adamson collies. The family is gone but their house and gardens still provide a unique record of the Malibu they once owned.

getty center

World-renowned museum with a
garden that is a living work of art

Bougainvillea adorns towering sheave-shaped bowers in Robert Irwin's garden at the Getty Center.

📞 (310) 440-7300
🕐 Open Tues–Wed 11am–7pm, Thurs–Fri 11am–9pm, Sat Sun 10am–6pm; closed Mondays and major holidays
$ Gardens and museum admission free via timed-entry ticket available on website; you must reserve in advance via website and pay for on-site parking (same-day use with Getty Villa) if you arrive by car
🚌 Public transportation
🐕 No dogs

Richard Meier, the architect of the Getty Center, hated Robert Irwin's garden. And Robert Irwin, the artist who created the Getty Center Central Garden, despised Richard Meier's architecture. I suppose one could charitably look upon this battle of two Godzilla-sized egos as a kind of yin and yang. Personally, I am on Irwin's side. The garden at the Getty Center is full of life, color, imagination, and movement. As for the museum buildings . . . well, when you visit the Getty Center, you can decide for yourself.

And visit you should, because the Getty Center, however you look at it, provides a unique cultural experience. The garden alone makes a trip there worthwhile, but you also get to enjoy the art collection (the star attraction likely being Van Gogh's *Irises*). The oil magnate J. Paul Getty bought 750 acres of a mountaintop for his museum complex and then proceeded to shave it down into five levels crowned by Meier's white, fortresslike buildings. There's definitely a sense of destination and arrival as you make your way by tram from the parking levels up to the entrance; it's like a Los Angeles version of the Acropolis.

You'll see Meier's version of a garden, courtesy of landscape architect Laurie Olin, in the Arrival Plaza: aerial hedges with razor-clipped sides, a lavender trellis with a white wisteria, pollarded sycamores. Stiff, controlled, subservient to the architecture, this is the sort of plantscape Meier would like to have seen everywhere at the Getty Center. Many of us are thankful he didn't get his way.

Let's move on to Robert Irwin's Central Garden. An installation artist associated with the Light and Space art movement of the 1960s, Irwin was sixty-four years old when he received the commission to design the Getty Center garden in 1992. It took five years to complete and was apparently a somewhat humbling experience, since Irwin didn't really know that much about garden plants and had to work closely with the landscape architecture firm Spurlock Poirier, as well as horticulturists, nurserymen, and the disapproving Meier. The Getty Center considers Irwin's work a copyrighted piece of art and officially describes it as "Mixed media (construction and plant materials), 134,000 sq. ft." A staff of forty gardeners keeps this art garden—and Laurie Olin's Cactus Garden, the other big garden at the Getty Center—in museum-quality shape. Because it is a work of art that uses water as an essential component, it is exempt from the drought-related water restrictions that have stopped the gush, flow, and trickle of most other fountains in California.

Irwin famously described his work for the Getty as "a sculpture in the form of a garden aspiring to be art." Think of it as an immersive experience that unfolds around you and engages all your senses. Irwin wanted the garden to be the natural antithesis of the forbidding structures behind it: there's no white, no square or geometric shapes; where steel is used it's meant to rust, not gleam. It's not as if Irwin reinvented the wheel here; the garden's basic elements—plants, stone, water—have been the building blocks of garden design for millennia. Like all gardens, this one is about color, shape, texture, and the interplay of plants with nature. There's no need to interpret anything. Just enjoy it, and know that it is one of the most meticulously groomed and cared for gardens in the world.

The first part of the garden is deceptively simple. A narrow, zigzagging pathway forces you to slow down, walk single file, pay attention. A stream flows down a culvertlike channel, filling the air with a quiet rush of sound. Five bridges cross the stream and at each bridge the course and sound of the water changes. You walk from full sunlight into the dappled shade of sycamores. Three times a year the gardeners are tasked with cutting off every other leaf to create the perfect dapple. Deer grass (*Muhlenbergia rigens*) is planted like a flowing undercurrent beneath the sycamores. There are other trees in the garden, too—dogwoods, crape myrtles, and paperbark maples—with different blossoms, bark textures, leaf shapes, and colors.

Next comes a zone of small plants with muted colors. As you continue down the path, the size of the plants increases and the

Robert Irwin's art garden at the Getty Center culminates in the Sunken Garden.

colors intensify. And when I say color, I mean *color*. Unlike the architect Meier, the artist Irwin was drawn to a mix of hot pinks, reds, purples, and oranges; nasturtium is his favorite color. You'll see lots of mirror plants (*Coprosma repens* 'Tequila Sunrise'), a tender evergreen with gorgeously colored leaves. When Irwin wanted to add a rose to his garden palette, he chose *Rosa* 'Trumpeter', the reddest of the red floribundas. And more color awaits you as the pathway descends to a plaza graced with three bougainvillea arbors. In recent summers, they have appeared a bit scrawny because of the drought, but the bright pink flowers trained up inside steel trellises that look like giant wheatsheaves are still an amazing sight.

Water flows through the bougainvillea plaza and cascades over a massive stone wall into an enormous pool. Planters in the center of the pool hold a breathtaking display of flowering plants—just one type per season—in an intricate design reminiscent of a Moorish pattern or Elizabethan knot garden. In the early spring you'll see pink-flowering dogwoods; red-flowered azaleas come later. A walkway leads around the pool, but you're always above it, looking down at the brilliantly colorful design against the backdrop of the stone wall with the cascading water. The cost of changing out these thousands of flowering plants every season and trucking them to nurseries where they spend the rest of the year is astronomical, to say the least. But that's the price you pay for having a world-class art garden viewed by thousands of visitors a day.

But wait, there's more! Actually, there's a lot more. Laurie Olin's landscaping for the rest of the museum campus complements the architecture but never challenges it, the way Irwin's garden does. Olin's most visible work is the Cactus Garden at the South Promontory. As you climb the stairs to reach it, you'll pass plantings of agave and bird of paradise (*Strelitzia reginae*, the official flower of Los Angeles). The spiny mounds and spiky columns of the Cactus Garden fill the long, reverse-P-shaped extension of the South Promontory. You can't get into the garden, but enjoy the view—all Los Angeles is spread out before you in the distance.

Laurie Olin's Cactus Garden at the Getty Center overlooks Los Angeles.

The dramatic Outer Peristyle garden at the Getty Villa in Malibu is an authentic re-creation of a Roman garden buried by the eruption of Mt. Vesuvius.

getty villa

17985 Pacific Coast Highway, Malibu, CA 90265
getty.edu/visit/villa
Visit year-round

....

- 📞 (310) 440-7300
- 🕐 Open Wed–Mon 10am–5pm, Sat 10am–9pm; closed Tuesdays and major holidays
- 💲 Admission free but timed-entry ticket required via website; parking fee (same-day use with Getty Center); reserve free tickets in advance
- 🐕 No dogs

Ancient Roman-style gardens re-created in a villa-museum in Malibu

If you've ever wondered what an ancient Roman garden looked like, the Getty Villa in Malibu offers a unique opportunity to see one. The villa opened in 1974, but its horticultural and architectural antecedents date back almost 2,000 years, specifically to 79 A.D. That's the year Mt. Vesuvius blew its top and buried the southern Italian cities of Pompeii and Herculaneum under a layer of volcanic ash. The ash hardened and preserved both cities, providing archaeologists with a comprehensive and unusually intimate view of Roman life in the first century.

J. Paul Getty visited these world-famous tourist sites near Naples in 1912 and was so impressed that he began to collect Roman antiquities. Several decades later, when he decided to build a museum to house this collection, he chose to reproduce the Villa dei Papiri (Villa of the Papyri) from Herculaneum as the setting for his treasures. Although it's been adapted to serve as a modern museum, the villa displays all the classic architectural features of a luxurious first-century Roman country house.

Re-creating a Roman garden of antiquity was a trickier proposition. Garden scenes painted on the walls of ancient Roman villas provided clues as to what plants the Romans used and how their gardens were laid out. Later, archeologists were able to identify specific plants based on the size of their excavated root cavities. Garden curators traveled to Italy to visit ancient garden sites and study the latest research. The result is that the gardens at the Getty Villa provide the finest example of an ancient Roman garden anywhere in the United States (and perhaps the world). Malibu's Mediterranean climate offers growing conditions similar to those of southern Italy, so the same plants that once graced the Villa dei Papiri can be seen at the Getty Villa.

The herbs and pollarded fruit trees in the long, walled, rectangular Herb Garden, the first garden you come to, served a variety of culinary, medicinal, and ritual needs. The mosaic of hardy perennials and colorful annuals includes mint, lemon balm, lovage, dittany, oregano, thyme, spearmint, apple mint, horsemint, lavender, bay leaf, rue, basil, chives, and walking onions. What the heck, you may ask, is a walking onion? Originally from Egypt, these miniature onions grow on the top of the stalk; when they mature, they pull the stalk down and, if soil conditions are right, set new plants—in other words, they "walk" across the garden. The tall, thistlelike plants in the Herb Garden are cardoons, related to globe artichokes; the Romans ate their braised stems. Costmary, an aromatic plant in the daisy family, was used as a bookmark in papyrus scrolls because it repels silverfish. Many of the plants in Roman gardens attracted bees and were important in the production of honey.

The Romans cultivated many apple and stone fruit trees that had been brought to Greece and the Mediterranean from the Far East by Alexander the Great as early as the fourth century B.C.: pomegranate, plum, olive, lemon, apple, peach, fig, pear, and apricot were all known to Roman gardeners. And we mustn't forget the grapes that put the *veritas* in Roman *vino*. The grape vines at the villa are trained on trellises made from alder grown along the Amalfi coast.

As you enter and explore the villa, you'll come upon three more gardens. They are defined by the site's symmetrical architecture and are themselves symmetrical, built within open peristyles (covered walkways). The Outer Peristyle, adjacent to the Herb Garden and entered from the villa's south doors, is the largest and most dramatic of the gardens. Though it's empty now (because of the drought), a 17-foot-deep and 220-foot-long pool forms the garden's centerpiece. The pool, blue as a slice of the Mediterranean, is surrounded by gravel pathways, circular stone benches,

Bronze civet heads adorn the central fountain in the Getty Villa's East Garden; theatrical masks and mosaic tiles decorate an adjacent wall fountain.

geometrical boxwood hedges, and lush plantings of flowers (violets, marigolds, roses), herbs (rosemary), woody shrubs (bay laurel, myrtle, oleanders), English ivy, and European fan palms. The Romans loved roses for their color, scent, and oils, and here you'll see the damasks and brilliant magenta campion roses grown in antiquity. Replicas of bronze sculptures found at the Villa dei Papiri are placed in their original locations. A peristyle with marble columns surrounds this formal garden and leads visitors past trompe l'oeil wall paintings to an outdoor gallery with views of the Pacific Ocean.

The more intimate Inner Peristyle is surrounded on all four sides by the villa's living quarters (now galleries in the museum). The narrow reflecting pool (recently reflecting nothing more than California's drought) is graced by bronze statues of women who look as though they might be dancing or casting magic spells, but are actually drawing and carrying water from a stream; their ivory inlayed eyes give them a spooky, supernatural look. The statues and square marble basins are replicas of finds from the Villa dei Papiri. Strips of boxwood and domes of rosemary enhance the symmetrical architecture and add a refreshing touch of green. If and when the pools in the two peristyle gardens are once again filled, the sparkling water will animate and add immeasurably to the beauty of the spaces.

Bronze statues re-created from Roman originals line the reflecting pool of the Inner Peristyle garden at the Getty Villa.

Water is also an integral component of the East Garden, a tranquil walled sanctuary found beyond the east stair of the museum. It still flows from the mouths of the sculpted bronze civets encircling the large basin fountain in the center of the garden, but the other fountain, built into the east wall and decorated with theatrical masks and mosaic tiles with sea shells, has been turned off. Shaded by sycamore and laurel trees, this peaceful haven was used exclusively by the family, and especially by the women of the household, who could come here to escape the busy comings and goings and business dealings that took place in the villa. It was the only place where they could enjoy privacy and quiet contemplation.

The gardens are integral to the whole experience of the Getty Villa, just as they were to the Villa dei Papiri almost 2,000 years ago. In that sense, they are timeless reminders of the aesthetic and utilitarian beauty that plants bring into our lives, wherever and whenever we live.

A pensive-looking bronze boy at the Getty Villa was re-created from an original Roman work from the first century A.D.

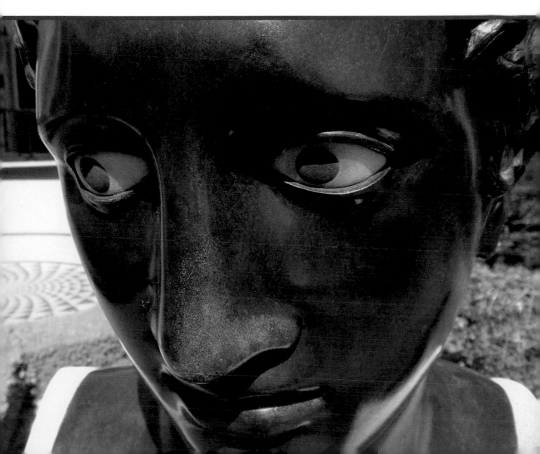

greystone mansion and gardens

905 Loma Vista Drive, Beverly Hills, CA 90210
greystonemansion.org
Visit year-round; April–September for roses

- 📞 (310) 285-6830
- 🕐 Grounds open daily 10am–5pm (6pm summer); closed Thanksgiving, Dec 25; house open only for special events
- $ Grounds admission free
- 🐕 Dogs on leash

Terraced formal gardens adorn
a massive estate wih a backstory
worthy of a Hollywood script

Though it doesn't have the botanical splendor or glamorous cachet of the nearby Virginia Robinson Gardens, this former Beverly Hills estate is worth a quick visit just to marvel at the size of the house—in all California, only Hearst Castle in San Simeon is larger—and to enjoy the remnants of its once-great gardens. Keep in mind, however, that the story behind Greystone is in some ways more compelling than what you'll find there today.

If you live in Southern California, you're probably aware of the name Doheny. Doheny Drive and Doheny Road in Beverly Hills, and Doheny State Beach in Orange County are all named for Edward L. Doheny (1856–1935), a Wisconsin-born wheeler-dealer who made history—and millions of dollars—when he struck oil in Los Angeles in 1892. Geysers of liquid gold in L.A. and later Mexico catapulted this scrappy Irish Catholic, who just a few years earlier didn't have money to pay his rent, into one of the world's richest men. In 1926 he bought 12.5 acres of undeveloped ranchland atop a lofty Beverly Hills ridge and gave it to his only son, Ned, as a belated wedding gift. A 46,000-square-foot mansion with landscaped grounds and gardens went with it. It took a year and a half to complete and cost Doheny over $3 million. To be fair, Ned did have to kick in ten bucks to "purchase" the place from his dad.

He may have been devout, but old man Doheny was hardly ethical when it came to his business dealings. He paid a $100,000 bribe to Albert Fall, U.S. Secretary of the Interior under Warren G. Harding, so that Fall would award him oil-drilling rights on a huge swath of federally owned land in Wyoming known as Teapot Dome. Ned and his childhood friend Theodore "Hugh" Plunkett were tapped to deliver the payola in a black valise. The bribe was discovered, Fall was sent to jail, and the Dohenys, father and son, were indicted, along with Hugh Plunkett. The Teapot Dome scandal, as it came to be known, remained the biggest U.S. government scandal until Watergate.

On the night of February 16, 1929, before Ned and Hugh Plunkett were scheduled to testify, and just months after Ned, his wife,

Strong architectural elements evoke Renaissance Italy at Greystone Mansion in Beverly Hills.

and five children finally moved into Greystone Mansion, Ned was shot to death in his new home by Plunkett, who then turned the gun on himself. That was the official story, at any rate. It's full of holes, so to speak, but if I spend any more time on this lurid murder-suicide, we'll never get to the gardens—or what's left of them.

As you walk down from the parking lot, you'll come to a terrace that offers the first glimpse of the grounds designed by the German-American landscape architect Paul Thiene (1880–1971). Thiene had been employed by the famous landscape firm Olmsted Brothers in Brookline, Massachusetts, until 1910, and probably came to Doheny's attention when Thiene worked on the 1915 Panama-California Exposition in San Diego's Balboa Park. For Greystone, Thiene laid out a series of formal terraces that took advantage of the magnificent views of Los Angeles (with Doheny's oil rigs visible in the distance) and adorned them with a hodge-podge of European garden styles. It's hard to classify the overall scheme except to say that it's neo, with neo-Gothic, neo-Renaissance, and neoclassical elements drawn from garden styles in Italy, France, and England. Fountains and pools added a further touch of romance, as did flowing brooks and a now-vanished 80-foot waterfall.

The first terrace you come to instantly evokes Renaissance Italy. Here you can see how Thiene's strong architectural elements defined the formal garden spaces. A plaza with a central fountain has wide steps that lead up to a higher view terrace with a stone balustrade lined with rapier-thin Italian cypresses. From here you descend to a lower level where a narrow, grassy allée runs between more cypresses and the upper terrace's massive stone wall. It looks like the thick defensive wall of a medieval castle in England or France.

From here, look down on the back of the enormous mansion designed by Gordon B. Kaufmann, a Southern California architect. The exterior, clad in Indiana limestone and roofed with Welsh slate, is somewhat dour. The opulence is all within. The fifty-five rooms feature oak and marble floors, hand-carved stone fireplaces, oak balustrades, and ceiling beams. There was a screening room, even a bowling alley. Unfortunately, you won't be able to see any of it unless you're attending a special event.

Make your way behind the house and through the giant court-yard to the front entrance. Stairs lead down to a double row of boxwood parterres planted with white roses beside the house. The

Boxwood parterres enclose rose beds at Greystone Mansion, once the largest residence in Los Angeles.

walkway ends at a long, lovely reflecting pool full of waterlilies and bordered by colorful begonias, a neoclassical exedra at the far end. The view from here extends all the way to Santa Monica Bay.

The last garden area to visit is the Formal Garden, located beside the first terrace you encountered. Here, a verdant green lawn is enclosed within a stone wall to the east and a carved balustrade to the west. A fountain murmurs on a geometric pavement at the north end. The garden has a quiet, almost cloistered feel.

The story of Greystone didn't end with Ned's murder and Hugh Plunkett's suicide. Lucy, Ned's widow, remarried and lived in the mansion until 1955. It was sold and resold and finally purchased by the City of Beverly Hills in 1965 so they could build a 19-million-gallon reservoir at the top of the property. In 1971, Doheny's original parcel and an additional three acres was turned into a public park. Once a verdant showplace, some of the property now looks sadly neglected. But the massive house and the gardens that remain are evocative reminders of the larger-than-life personalities and rags-to-riches stories on which Los Angeles was built. Film buffs take note: the character Daniel Day-Lewis plays in *There Will Be Blood* is loosely based on Edward Doheny.

mildred e. mathias botanical garden

UCLA campus, 777 Tiverton Drive, Los Angeles, CA 90095
botgard.ucla.edu
Visit year-round; April and May for flowering cacti and
maximum blooms

··

- 📞 (310) 825-1260
- 🕐 Open Mon–Fri 8am–5pm, Sat–Sun and winter 8am–
  4pm; closed university holidays
- $ Admission free
- ♿ Some steep steps not suitable for wheelchairs; finding
  a close parking spot is difficult, and parking rules are
  strictly enforced
- 🚌 Public transportation
- 🐕 No dogs

Exotic collections and rare specimens abound in a newly revitalized research garden

Whenever I visit this seven-acre botanical garden on the UCLA campus in central L.A., I feel like I'm entering a wonderful old library, one that's crowded with rare plants instead of books. Established in 1929, the garden is loaded with decades' worth of tropical and subtropical species that reflect the ongoing research and horticultural interests of UCLA faculty and students. It's dense and even junglelike in places, and you never know what you'll find around the next corner.

The garden was built on an arroyo—a dry, steep-sided canyon with a creek running through it—back when much of L.A. was still undeveloped. The land was originally covered with coastal sage scrub, the tough, drought-resistant plants native to this part of Southern California. Those plants were removed to make way for new plants from around the world. The garden's first manager, the aptly named George C. Groenewegen (which means "greenways"), put out a "plants wanted" call to other botanical gardens and collections throughout California. Even the U.S. Department of Agriculture donated specimens. Before twenty years had passed, the garden had about 1,500 species and varieties. That number soon expanded to over 3,500.

As it grew, the garden planted more and more trees, including many species of figs (*Ficus*) and eucalyptus that later became mainstays of California landscaping. (Little did they know that horticultural opinion would eventually turn against Australian eucalyptus, which are today considered something of invasive pests.) By the 1950s, the garden also had special sections devoted to succulents, aquatics, camellias, and gymnosperms (conifers, ginkgos, cycads). One of the largest Torrey pines in the United States makes its home here, as does a 160-foot-tall *Eucalyptus grandis*, giant bamboo, and a cinnamon tree from southeast Asia. The garden also has four dawn redwoods (*Metasequoia glyptostroboides*), a deciduous redwood thought to be extinct until it was discovered in a remote valley in China in 1941. The garden was among the first in the United States to receive seeds.

Feathery Australian tree ferns and a collection of primitive cycads give parts of the Mildred E. Mathias Botanical Garden at UCLA a tropical look.

The garden's many palm trees give it a dense, exotic overlay. The palm collection on Pine and Palm Hill and scattered throughout the grounds features over fifty species, including windmill palms (the wood used for construction in China), *Corypha* species from southeast Asia, Canary Island date palms, and Asian fishtail palms that flower once and then die. The Chilean wine palms, now threatened in their native habitat, bleed sap that is used to make palm honey and palm wine.

As you wander along the shady paths on the west side of the arroyo, you'll encounter a fern collection with terrestrial, arboreal, and aquatic species, and a bromeliad garden with a diverse collection of plants from Hawaii. Obtaining plants with exotic blooms, like Hawaiian hibiscus, was part of the collecting strategy in the garden's earlier years.

Not everything here is rare or exotic. The habitat garden, used as a living classroom for students to learn the importance of habitat creation and conservation, displays over a hundred species of common plants like echinaceas, buddleias, milkweeds, salvias, and chocolate flower (*Berlandiera lyrata*) that attract birds and benefit butterflies, moths, and insects.

The scene changes on the east side of the garden, where the dry, sunny slopes are given over to native California plants (like that Torrey pine) and the desert garden with desert willows, ocotillos, and huge euphorbias. A grass tree with pom-poms of flowering green stalks, and a lovely, purple-flowering lilac vine (*Hardenbergia violacea*) are Australian imports. The *Ephedra tweediana* from South America is an interesting shrub with a grasslike mass of leaves on thin, wiry, flexible branches. I particularly like the fact that when plants blossom in this garden, and lots of them do, sometimes spectacularly, the dead flowers aren't trimmed off. It lets you see the entire life cycle of the plant.

The garden is named for Dr. Mildred Mathias (1906–1995), who served as director from 1956 to 1974. This Missouri-born botanist was a pioneer in her field and a tireless researcher and educator who became a leading botanist and conservationist in America. In the early 1960s, she was one of the first to decry the destruction of the tropical rain forests and in 1964, when the field of ethnopharmacology was in its infancy, she went on expeditions to Amazonian Peru and Ecuador, Tanganyika, and Zanzibar to collect and screen plants of tropical forests for new medicines, learning about the properties of certain plants from native

Fruiting pomegranate trees are among the many botanical delights to be found at the Mildred E. Mathias Botanical Garden.

herbalists and medicine men. Her efforts as a conservationist won her many prestigious awards, and after retiring, she continued to lead research groups to the tropics. Mathias made her last trip to Costa Rica in 1994, when she was eighty-eight years old, and was planning another one when she died the following year. It's dedicated botanists and plant lovers like Mildred Mathias who today use the garden as a living plant laboratory.

virginia robinson gardens

The first garden estate in Beverly
Hills features lavish gardens
and a historic mansion

1008 Elden Way, Beverly Hills, CA 90210
robinsongardens.org
Visit year-round; January and February for camellias and
azaleas; April–July for roses; November–June for
clearest ocean views

- 📞 (310) 550-2087
- 🕐 Open for docent-led tours only, Tues–Sat at 10am and
1pm, by advance reservation
- $ Admission fee
- ♿ Stairways in some parts of the garden not suitable for
wheelchairs
- 🐕 No dogs

Above the Lily Pond
is the ornate, Beaux-
Arts–style Pool
Pavilion at the Virginia
Robinson Gardens.

Touring this century-old Beverly Hills estate is a highlight among
Southern California house and garden experiences, but you need
to make a reservation at least two weeks in advance. Once inside
the gates, you'll be treated to a fascinating glimpse of a golden age
that lives on in this most elegant of garden settings.

To understand this estate and what it represents in California's
cultural and horticultural history, you have to know a bit about
Harry and Virginia Robinson, the power couple who created it.
Virginia Dryden was a Missouri-born belle who moved to Los
Angeles with her family in 1880, long before Hollywood became a
mecca for moviemaking. In 1903 she married her neighbor, Harry
Robinson, heir to the Robinson department store chain. Fast forward a few years: Harry inherits the Robinson chain, it expands
into the Robinsons-May company and eventually, after Harry's
death, with Virginia as chairman, morphs into Macy's. Retail has
its rewards.

After a three-year honeymoon in Europe, India, and Kashmir,
Harry and Virginia returned to Los Angeles and bought a 15-acre
parcel of land in the treeless lima-bean fields that would eventually become Beverly Hills. The sloping land offered a vista of the
Pacific Ocean, seven miles away, and Catalina Island. Virginia's
architect father was hired to design the 6,000-square-foot neoclassical Italianate villa they called home for the rest of their lives.
In 1911, when they moved in, you could say Beverly Hills was born.

So were the gardens. Both Virginia and Harry were avid gardeners—Virginia once said she was "almost a professional gardener"—and were inspired by the plants and gardens they saw
on their world travels. When you visit this historic estate today,
it's difficult to believe that the lush array of mature tropical and

semi-tropical plants and trees hasn't always been here. But the gardens were started entirely from scratch, often from seeds or cuttings.

Throughout their tenure, the Robinsons obtained horticultural advice from landscape architects, important nurserymen, and influential friends. One garden consultant worked for the director Cecil B. DeMille, another for their neighbors, Walt and Lillian Disney. There's a sense of drama and theatricality in the gardens, to be sure, but it's generous and assured rather than vulgar and over-the-top. These gardens were, after all, not created just for quiet repose; for decades they were the scene of glamorous Hollywood parties on a lavish scale.

The Front Garden was the first to be planted. It's still graced by the Southern magnolia and tulip magnolia trees that were planted in the 1920s. White and purple wisteria drapes the porch where Virginia liked to be photographed when the flowers were in bloom. The tall organ pipe cactus (*Cereus peruvianus*) on one side of the porch was given to Virginia as a gift in a five-gallon pot; it blooms only at night, producing large, fragrant white flowers that have a very short shelf life. The bay laurel and Himalayan laurel hedges are fragrant, too. The gold medallion tree (*Cassia leptophylla*), at its showiest in the spring, was planted by the Los Angeles Board of Supervisors in 1976, to commemorate Virginia's plan to gift her house and gardens to the County of Los Angeles; she died the following year.

The tour includes a visit to the main rooms in the villa, still furnished as they were when the Robinsons began to host their famous dinner parties and galas. To say that Virginia ran a tight ship is an understatement. In her household, the protocol used was the same as at the White House. Every Wednesday there was a black-tie dinner for twenty-one, with food prepared by her Cordon Bleu–trained chef. The guest list for larger parties and benefits could reach 400. Every summer, to kick off the Los Angeles Philharmonic's summer season at the Hollywood Bowl, the orchestra would come to the Robinsons' and repeat their opening-night concert on the Great Lawn for hundreds of guests.

That Great Lawn, the scene of so many Hollywood parties, unfurls like a long green carpet behind the house. This second garden area extends from the back terrace of the villa to the Pool Pavilion, and is enclosed by high brick walls punctuated by Italian cypress trees that add to its look of Anglo-Mediterranean

Virginia and Harry Robinson's pink-curtained dining room overlooks the magnificent Palm Forest.

symmetry. The borders along the walls are planted with an eye- and nose-catching array of perennials that include old-fashioned, sweetly scented favorites like *Rosa* 'Joseph's Coat', orange and yellow Cape honeysuckles (*Tecoma capensis* and *T. capensis* 'Aurea'), and Madagascar jasmine (*Stephanotis floribunda*). Virginia loved trees and would collect seeds or starts of special trees she encountered on her travels. The red powder-puff tree (*Calliandra haematocephala*), with its year-round display of red puffs, and the cockspur coral tree (*Erythrina crista-galli*) were two of her favorites.

The blue-tiled pool at the far end of the Great Lawn is raised just enough so that you don't see it from the house or even from the lawn. What you do see is the Lily Pond below and, above it, the ornate Beaux-Arts–style Pool Pavilion, built in 1925. In this rarefied world, guests could come by for a game of tennis—Virginia once played against Charlie Chaplin—and relax by the pool afterward. In 2015, two side panels of grass beside the Pool Pavilion were replaced with species of *Dymondia*, a drought-tolerant genus of South African plants in the daisy family, with dark leaves and bright yellow flowers. Other lawn areas will be replanted with pink vinca from Madagascar that requires watering only once a week.

West of the Great Lawn, a series of descending brick terraces takes you into the Italian Terrace Garden. Thanks to Southern California's Mediterranean climate, an enormous variety of trees and plants grows on these sunny slopes, but the overall design and the presence of Italian cypress and olive trees, rosemary bushes, bay laurel hedges, and fragrant cistus immediately evoke the old hillside gardens of Tuscany and the Amalfi coast.

In the camellia collection near the top terrace, have a look at 'Coco', the white camellia named for Coco Chanel, one of Virginia's favorite couturiers. The Musical Stairs, so-called because of the murmuring water that flows in a channel down their center, lead down to the Lion Terrace, guarded by two Italian stone lions. As you descend and explore this area, you'll find a citrus grove and numerous fruit trees, including persimmon, loquat, pineapple guava, apple, mulberry, avocado, and pomegranate (used as a hedge).

The showstopping coral-red bougainvillea trained along a fence at the end of the tennis court came from a start Virginia brought back from South Africa. You'll pass it on your way to the Palm Forest, the final highlight of this remarkable estate. Here, brick paths wind through the largest grove of king palms outside Australia. Harry and Virginia started this amazing collection from a few seeds or saplings imported from Queensland; the trees, now endangered in their native habitat, have flourished in Beverly Hills and reseeded themselves to make a forest.

An antique Italian urn resides in a field of asphodels at Virginia Robinson Gardens.

Harry was only fifty-four when he died, but Virginia lived to be ninety-nine, and never left the house and gardens she created. She would go for a walk twice a day, accompanied by her major-domo, and right up to the end there was hell to pay if she encountered a hose left out after watering.

The Lily Ponds were the first gardens at the Huntington estate in San Marino.

pasadena
& vicinity

descanso gardens

Informal urban retreat noted
for camellias, oak trees, roses,
lilacs—and its beauty in winter

1418 Descanso Drive, La Cañada Flintridge, CA 91011
descansogardens.org
Visit year-round; January and February for camellias; March–
    May for tulips, iris, lilacs; May–September for roses

A favorite greenspace for locals, Descanso Gardens is a former estate transformed into a "museum of living collections."

☎ (818) 949-4200
🕐 Open daily 9am–5pm; closed Dec 25
$ Admission fee
🐕 No dogs

Descanso Gardens is wonderful to visit at any time of year, but it is positively unforgettable in the winter. Beginning in January, while much of the nation shivers under snowdrifts or slogs through winter rains, the camellias at Descanso put on a show that will take your breath away.

Located in the San Rafael Hills, only fifteen miles and fifteen minutes from downtown Los Angeles, Descanso is a 160-acre botanical garden with a welcoming, informal feel. Locals use it as a kind of Central Park—a place to stroll, relax, or take a run, and its host of botanical treasures and colorful seasonal displays draws visitors from all over. Give yourself at least an hour and a half for a leisurely see-everything stroll.

Like many of the other botanical gardens in Southern California, Descanso was once a private estate. The land was purchased in 1936 by a character named E. Manchester Boddy (1891–1967), a self-made man who hoisted himself up from poverty to become owner and editor of the gritty and influential Los Angeles *Daily News*. Boddy was one of those nonstop hustlers whose energies and interests never seemed to flag. He worked as a miner, a ditch-digger, a New York City subway guard, and a salesman for the Encyclopaedia Britannica before moving to Los Angeles for his health (he'd been gassed in World War I). Under his leadership, the *Daily News* became the only newspaper in L.A. to report on crime and corruption. But this character's own character darkened when, in 1950, he entered politics and ran as a Republican candidate for senator against Helen Gahagan Douglas. During the rancorous campaign, Boddy resorted to calling Douglas a "pink lady" or "red hot"—insinuating that she was a Communist. He lost to Douglas in the primary, but Douglas in turn lost to Richard Nixon, who used Boddy's "Red Scare" smear tactic in his own campaign.

When Boddy bought his oak-covered retreat in La Cañada, he named it Rancho del Descanso (Restful Ranch) and commissioned James Dolena, the so-called architect to the stars, to design a 12,000-square-foot, 22-room mansion in Dolena's signature Hollywood Regency style. The famed camellia collection took root in 1942 when Boddy purchased the Mission Nursery in San Gabriel to aid the owners, the Yoshimura family, who had been interned along with other Japanese-Americans during World War II. (Most interned Japanese-Americans lost their farms, homes, and businesses during this time.) When he purchased the nursery, all the nursery stock, including a large collection of camellias, came with it. Today the Descanso camellia collection is the largest in the country, with over 35,000 plants.

In 1953, Boddy sold Rancho del Descanso to Los Angeles County to keep the land from becoming the first Disneyland

The colorful wildflower garden at Descanso Gardens attracts bees and butterflies.

theme park. Soon after, a nonprofit group, the Descanso Gardens Guild, began a program to shape the future of this urban oasis. Today the garden has many updated features, such as the visitor center with its outdoor Descanso Café and gift shop, but the pleasure of Descanso is that you often feel like you're strolling through a timeless California landscape.

The Center Circle demonstration garden near the entrance gate changes its focus every few years. Its current look and plant palette is in keeping with California's growing awareness of the necessity for water-wise gardening. Using California natives and colorful, drought-tolerant plants from other Mediterranean regions, this eye-catching garden requires less than half the water that would be slurped up by a lawn. Everything in it, from the permeable hardscape to the irrigation system, is geared to water conservation.

From there, the wide Promenade runs southwest and loops through the property. In the spring, this area is ablaze with thousands of tulips. The five-acre Rose Garden graces the west side of the Promenade. Over 3,000 species, including heirloom roses and modern varieties from regions throughout the world, are displayed in different themed gardens, including most All-America Rose Selection (AARS) winners since 1940.

The Oak Woodland southwest of the Rose Garden re-creates a portion of the original Los Angeles Basin landscape of meadow, woodland, and chaparral. Shrubs, perennials, grasses, and oaks were all part of a native plant community that's rarely seen nowadays because of urban (over)development. In one part of the woodland, you'll find a lake with a bird observation station.

A pathway connects the Oak Woodland to the California Natives section, another of the landscapes that give Descanso its pleasantly natural ambience. This eight-acre garden was planted in 1959, making Descanso a Southern California pioneer in showcasing the state's native plant communities. Spring and early summer are the best times to see the natives in flower—standouts include yellow California flannelbush, white matilija poppies, mountain lilac, red monkey flower, and aromatic sage.

Descanso's newest garden, called Ancient Forest, is located in a grove of redwoods at the south end of the California Natives section. It highlights the oldest known plants on earth—ginkgos, tree ferns, redwoods, magnolias and, most notably, a collection of 150 cycads—all of them living fossils from the age of the dinosaurs. The palmlike cycads, many of them now endangered in their native habitats, were donated to Descanso in 2015 and are the stars of this garden.

The looping main path brings you next to the Oak Forest, divided into west and east sections. This is where you'll find the famed camellia collection. The tree-sized beauties grow beneath a canopy of 150-year-old coast live oaks.

Boddy's home—now a house-museum—sits on the east side of the Oak Forest. The architectural features are original but the interior decor is an updated interpretation of 1930s and 1940s style. Check out the Sturt Haaga Gallery near the house, with its rotating art shows, and make sure you have a look at the botanical work of art just outside the gallery: a beautiful and ingeniously constructed vertical wall garden planted with subtly shaded sedums.

Continuing north, back toward the entrance, you'll come to the Lilac Garden, at its fragrant best from mid-March to early May. The lilac collection at Descanso features more than 400 plants and about 250 varieties in shades of purple, magenta, pink, violet, and white. An early project of the Descanso Gardens Guild, the Lilac Garden began in 1953 with just one hybrid, *Syringa ×hyacinthiflora* 'Lavender Lady'. By 1965, Descanso's hybrid lilacs were being introduced to the nursery trade and had been sent to the National Arboretum in Washington, D.C. Not all the lilacs are fragrant, but when the conditions are right you'll get a noseful of their heady perfume.

The last garden highlight at Descanso is the one-acre Japanese Garden on the east side of the visitor center. This isn't an authentic Japanese garden such as you'd find in Portland or Seattle, but it evokes Japanese style with an arched bridge, koi-filled stream, tea house, and a traditional Japanese farmhouse called a *minka*. The plants are those associated with Japanese and Asian gardens: cherry and plum trees and azaleas that blossom in the spring, Japanese maples that turn shades of red and orange in the fall, and bamboo.

huntington library, art collections, and botanical gardens

1151 Oxford Road, San Marino, CA 91108
huntington.org
Visit year-round; January and February for cacti, camellias, roses; spring for flowering trees; summer for lotus and waterlilies

....

Completed in 2015, the new entrance gardens at the Huntington were designed to showcase colorful and drought-tolerant California native plants.

📞 (626) 405-2100
🕐 Open Memorial Day–Labor Day, Wed–Mon 10:30am–4:30pm; rest of the year Mon, Wed, Thurs noon–4:30pm, Fri–Sun 10:30am–4:30pm; closed major holidays
$ Admission fee
🚌 Public transportation
🐕 No dogs

World-class gardens with historic plant collections, at the Pasadena area's premier library-museum complex

For sheer eyepopping splendor, the gardens at the Huntington Library have no equal in California. That's a mighty tall claim but it happens to be true. Visiting the plant collections at the Huntington is not unlike perusing masterpieces in different galleries at a great art museum. In fact, there *are* art museums on the grounds, and a renowned library with a collection of rare books and manuscripts. After strolling through the 150 acres of landscaped gardens, you can pop in to see Gainsborough's famous *Blue Boy* or pore over a Shakespeare folio. Translation: give yourself as much time as you can, preferably half a day.

So who do we have to thank for this literary, artistic, and botanical bonanza? Henry E. Huntington (1850–1927) was the nephew of Collis Huntington, builder of the transcontinental railroad line that later became the Southern Pacific. Henry held executive positions in the company and, when his uncle died, consolidated his own interests by divorcing his wife and marrying Collis's much-younger trophy widow, Arabella. Yes, that means he married his aunt. Yes, there was a scandal. Though born in New York, Henry saw Southern California as the golden land of opportunity. He built the Pacific Electric Railway (the Red Line) and developed the Los Angeles neighborhoods it served. At fifty, he retired and turned his attention to the 600-acre ranch in San Marino that would become his legacy, the Huntington Library, Art Collections, and Botanical Gardens.

Huntington was a voracious collector of art, books, and plants. When it came to planning and planting his gardens, he was lucky to enlist the talents of William Hertrich (1878–1966), a German-born landscape gardener who spent over forty years helping to collect rare plants and supervise the installation of Huntington's now magnificently mature gardens.

You can make a looping "highlights tour" of all the major gardens in about two hours. Begin your journey at the new visitor center and entrance court, a $60 million project that opened in 2015. There's an introductory film, a noteworthy café, and a big museum shop in this area, but the new gardens are the real showstoppers—or show-starters, since you'll pass through them to reach all the other gardens. Designed by landscape architect Cheryl Barton, the new entrance gardens are a tapestry of low-growing, drought-tolerant Mediterranean plants contained within raised, rectangular beds bisected by narrow water channels that flow into terminal pools. These gardens are simple and elegant, and reflect the new water awareness seen in gardens throughout California.

Just south, you'll encounter the Palm Garden, where the thick trunks of stately tropical trees rise up like pillars amid a lush carpet of green. This was among the garden's first collections, and an early planting was a towering Canary Island date palm that Huntington rescued from his uncle Collis's home after it was destroyed in the 1906 San Francisco earthquake. (That tree is in the northwest corner of the adjacent Desert Garden; other palms in the collection are in the Jungle Garden.) Like all the gardens at the Huntington, the Palm Garden began as an experiment; many of the early specimens succumbed to frost, but by the late 1930s, Hertrich had amassed a vigorous collection of 450 palms from California, Europe, and Japan, later augmented by new additions like the rare and endangered Chilean wine palm (*Jubaea chilensis*), prized for its sweet sap.

South of the Palm Garden is what I consider to be the Huntington's greatest botanical treasure, the Desert Garden. Begun in 1907, this ten-acre garden is one of the oldest and largest collections of cacti and succulents in the world, with over 5,000 species in sixty landscaped beds. Hertrich collected the first specimens

Do Not Enter

from deserts in the Southwest and Mexico. Many of the golden barrel cactus were started from seed before 1915. The colors throughout this prickly paradise are always vibrant, but they are positively on fire during the winter blooming season. Prickly pears blossom with bright yellow flowers; red, flamelike blooms burst from the ocotillos; and rare bromeliads from Chile, *Puya alpestris* and *P. chilensis*, put on a spectacular show of blue-green and chartreuse flowers. The size of some of the specimens is overwhelming, from the 60-foot *Yucca filifera* and the odd boojum tree (*Fouquieria columnaris*) from Baja California, to the 20-ton, tree-sized *Cereus xanthocarpus*. Continue into the Desert Garden Conservatory to see aloes, euphorbias, living stones (*Lithops*), pincushion cacti (*Mammillaria*), and epiphytes.

Located west of the Desert Garden, the Lily Ponds are the oldest gardens at the Huntington. In 1904, William Hertrich transformed a mucky gully into this lush four-acre garden with two large and three small ponds filled with and surrounded by aquatic plants. This is a quiet, romantic spot with floating waterlilies and erect, summer-flowering pink-and-white lotus. A remarkable collection of bamboo—over seventy-five kinds—grows in dense groves around the ponds. The bronze statue of St. Francis was sculpted in 1924 by Clara Huntington, Henry's daughter.

Depending on your interests, you might want to explore the Australian Garden, the Subtropical Garden, the Jungle Garden, the Herb Garden, the Shakespeare Garden, or the delightfully old-fashioned Rose Garden. Some 3,000 roses, most of them old varieties from the eighteenth and nineteenth century, bloom here from March to Thanksgiving. This three-acre garden features a trellised promenade and, nearby, an eighteenth-century French stone *tempietto* ("small temple") that houses a suitably romantic statue entitled *Love, the Captive of Youth*, surrounded by a bed of *Rosa* 'Passionate Kisses'. Bring a fan to cool your ardor.

After the Rose Garden, the century-old Japanese Garden is probably the most popular garden at the Huntington. It's one of the oldest Japanese-style gardens in the nation, but it's not what you'd call authentic. It was created in an era (1928) when collecting and putting together various Japanese garden elements (such as the moon bridge) took precedence over creating a historically accurate Japanese garden landscape. Still, the Japanese Garden is wonderfully photogenic and contains a ceremonial teahouse and a traditional Japanese house that was created in Tokyo in 1904 and reassembled here. Superb examples of bonsai are displayed in the garden's Zen Court.

The North Vista at the Huntington, seen here in July with agapanthus in bloom, is lined with statues and has a backdrop of flowering camellias in the spring.

The newer Chinese Garden, called the Garden of Flowing Fragrance, should definitely not be missed. Covering 12.5 acres, it is among the largest Chinese gardens outside China. Unlike the walled, urban Chinese gardens in Portland and Vancouver, B.C., the Garden of Flowing Fragrance is open and expansive. Built in 2009 by architects and artisans from Suzhou, China's famed garden city, the Huntington's Chinese Garden strictly adheres to the traditional elements found in all Chinese gardens: water, plants, rocks, and architecture in the form of pavilions, bridges, and walkways. Fantastically shaped limestone rocks mined from Lake Tai near Suzhou surround the manmade lake, with its arched bridge and elaborate Pavilion of the Three Friends (those three friends are pine, bamboo, and flowering plum, all found nearby). The garden is set amid a grove of coast live oaks with underplantings of camellias. Gardens like this date from the Ming dynasty and were typically attached to the private homes of scholars, poets, and government officials. They were meant to be viewed as a series of carefully composed scenes offering reflections of harmony and beauty.

But there's another garden I want you to visit before you go. It's called the North Vista, and it's located behind the Huntington mansion, now a museum devoted to British and European art. Modeled after the great landscape parks in France and England, this vista unfurls as a vast green lawn enclosed on two sides by giant coast live oaks and at the end by a fountain. Playful and romantic eighteenth-century French sculptures are placed at regular intervals along the lawn, close to the trees. Planted under the trees is the Huntington's outstanding collection of camellias—or a large part of it, anyway. If you can, visit in January or February when the camellias are in bloom—it's an unforgettable sight. The botanical collections include nearly eighty different species camellias, many of them rare and historic, and some 1,200 cultivars. Descendants of some of the earliest camellias to arrive in England from Asia in the eighteenth century are represented here, including *Camellia japonica* 'Alba Plena' (with formal, white double blooms), and *C. reticulata* 'Captain Rawes' (bearing large, semi-double, rose-pink flowers). Also look for the large rose-red flowers of *C. japonica* 'California', which arrived on a Japanese steamer in 1888 and is believed to be the oldest camellia on record in Southern California.

los angeles county arboretum and botanic garden

Popular park and cultural center with interesting theme gardens and educational features

There's something for everyone in this 111-acre botanic garden in the San Gabriel Valley, about forty minutes northeast of central L.A. It's a big and pleasantly roamable place, popular with local residents who use it as a park, learning center, and cultural venue. And, like just about every other California garden of note, a complex past preceded its colorful present.

This land was inhabited over 3,000 years ago by the Tongva people, who called it Aleupkigna, "the place of many waters," because of its natural springs and sag ponds. The grasses, flowers, leaves, and roots of the indigenous coastal sage scrub habitat were integral to the Tongva, who used the bounty in many different forms. When the Spanish arrived, the Tongva were enslaved under the Spanish mission system and became forced laborers on a huge agricultural outpost of the San Gabriel Mission. Aleupkigna became Rancho Santa Anita and the Tongva became known as Gabrielinos. A Scotsman married to a Gabrielino woman became the first private owner of Rancho Santa Anita in 1840. From then until 1875, when the land was purchased for $200,000 by Elias "Lucky" Baldwin, the ranch went through several owners. Baldwin was the only one who left a visible mark—in the form of a Queen Anne–style mansion that sits near Baldwin Lake, created by Baldwin from one of the ancient ponds. The peacocks

301 North Baldwin Avenue, Arcadia, CA 91007
arboretum.org
Visit year-round; January and February for cactus and aloe
blooms

....

- 📞 (626) 821-3222
- 🕐 Open daily 9am–5pm; walking tours Tues–Fri 10am, Sat
  10:30am
- $ Admission fee
- 🐕 No dogs

Elias "Lucky" Baldwin
built this Queen
Anne–style mansion
on land that today
is the Los Angeles
County Arboretum
and Botanic Garden.

Bismarck palms, which are endemic to Madagascar, are among the attractions at the Los Angeles County Arboretum and Botanic Garden.

that roam the grounds and call from the trees are another memento from Lucky's days, descendants of the first peafowl to be imported into the continental United States in 1879. Baldwin, who eventually owned more than 40,000 acres of land in Los Angeles County, is remembered as the founder of the town of Arcadia, which he touted as a tourist resort, and the famed Santa Anita Race Track. Baldwin Hills, Mt. Baldwin, and Baldwin Avenue are some of the places named for him. By 1880, this Ohio-born businessman was so rich, it was said, that he didn't have to run after women, women ran after him. After four marriages, countless scandals, and two attempts on his life, which he continued to live at full tilt, Lucky Baldwin died at his home here in 1909. After his death, when oil was discovered, Rancho Santa Anita began pumping out an eighth of California's crude oil. In 1947 the State of California and the County of Los Angeles jointly purchased 111 acres of Rancho Santa Anita, née Aleupkigna, and founded the Los Angeles County Arboretum.

That's the short version of a long story. But it's not the end, by any means. This is a garden that keeps growing, both in terms of its plant material and horticultural and community outreach. By 1949, the first greenhouse had been built. Two years later, the first 1,000 trees were planted. The arboretum opened to the public in 1956. In the ensuing decades, more greenhouses were constructed, most notably the Tropical Greenhouse (1975–76), and more special garden areas were planned and planted, including the popular Prehistoric Forest.

Give yourself about an hour and a half to two hours if you want to make a circuit and have a look at everything. You can pick up a map at the visitor center when you enter. A host of smaller display and specialty gardens are clustered along the main path heading north from the entrance. The Weaver's Garden features plants used around the world to weave mats, fabrics, benches, even houses. The Carnivorous Plants/Epiphyllum Collection showcases insect-eating plants, while the Tropical Greenhouse displays exotic orchids (it's among the country's largest orchid collections) as well as primitive cycads native to Mexico and almost extinct in the wild. More familiar domestic gardens along this central pathway include the large Organic Vegetable Garden with a 4,400-gallon rainwater harvester and an orchard with apple, plum, peach, papaya, guava, citrus, and pomegranate trees. These gardens obviously serve an educational function (never assume a modern child knows where a vegetable or fruit comes from), but are lovely in their own right.

At the end of this collection of gardens, head down the marked Serpent Trail, a curving pathway that leads you through a series of gardens loaded with fascinating plants and trees from Australia, Madagascar, and Africa. Distinctive drought-tolerant trees along the route include three native to Queensland, Australia: the Queensland bottle tree (*Brachychiton rupestris*), so-called because of its bulbous lower trunk; the Queensland kauri pine (*Agathis robusta*), found only in Queensland and Papua, New Guinea; and the foxtail palm (*Wodyetia bifurcata*) with drooping bushy fronds (this tree was relatively unknown until 1978). My favorite trees in this area are the Bismarck palms (*Bismarckia nobilis*) from Madagascar, with their short and rather stumpy trunks and stiff, fanlike fronds. There are also different varieties of myrtles, eucalyptus, and acacias to be seen.

More notable plant collections are located near the southeast corner of the Africa section. The most dramatic are the Desert Display Garden and the Aloe Trail; both typically hit their peak blooming season in January and February. Enormous specimens of *Aloe candelabrum* line the path, along with plantings of yellow-flowered resin spurge (*Euphorbia resinifera*), and other cactus-looking euphorbias.

South of the Bauer Lawn and Fountains in the center of the arboretum is what's called the Historic Circle. The dense Prehistoric Forest forms the north end of the circle, which includes Baldwin Lake and a collection of restored historic structures. The oldest is the 1840 adobe that was the first building to be erected on Rancho Santa Anita when it passed into private ownership. Docents lead tours through the large and airy Queen Anne Cottage, a white clapboard with red decorative trim, that was Lucky Baldwin's home from 1885 until his death; if you miss the tour, enjoy a rest stop in one of the wicker chairs on the wraparound porch.

The Grace Kallam Perennial Garden to the west side of the circle is a lovely color-themed perennial garden shaded by purple-leaved redbuds (*Cercis canadensis* 'Forest Pansy') and a Chinese fringe tree (*Chionanthus retusus*). This area, called Meadowbrook, also has a collection of daylilies and magnolias. Continue south and you'll hear the refreshing splash of the Meyberg Waterfall as it cascades past an array of hardy tropical and temperate plants. On the knoll behind the waterfall you can visit a grove of oak trees and the arboretum's ficus collection.

The last time I visited, a trio of brightly gowned young women dressed as princesses from Walt Disney fairytales passed by. I have no idea what they were doing or why they were there, but the sight of them lent an enchanted air to a place once called "the fairy spot of the Valley."

rancho santa ana botanic garden

Largest botanic garden in the state
dedicated to California native plants

📞 (909) 625-8767
🕐 Open daily 8am–5pm, closed major holidays; many
   different kinds of guided tours are available, including
   birding and wildflower walks and a monthly tram tour;
   see website for details
$ Admission fee
🐕 No dogs

Joshua trees are among the California native plants found at Rancho Santa Ana Botanic Garden.

The lushly planted gardens that we see and enjoy in California today haven't been around all that long. A hundred years ago, much of the Southern California landscape, where it wasn't used for ranching, grazing, or farming, was still coastal chaparral and sage scrublands. As the state's population exploded and development usurped more and more land, the native plant species that had adapted themselves to this Mediterranean-type climate started to disappear at an alarming rate.

Though many public gardens in California have a native plant section, those that concentrate exclusively on the state's indigenous flora are rarer than the Catalina Island mountain mahogany (*Cercocarpus traskiae*), of which only seven specimens now remain in the wild. That fact alone should tell you why Rancho Santa Ana is important. This botanic garden plays an important role in finding, saving, growing, cataloguing, and preserving plants from all four zones of the California Floristic Province. Botanically speaking, those four zones cover the entire state and extend into the southern part of Oregon, east into Nevada, and south into Baja, Mexico. The range of California plants displayed at Rancho Santa Ana is huge—about 2,000 taxa—but the focus is on Southern California and Baja.

The loss of native plant habitat was noted by Susanna Bixby Bryant as early as the 1920s. A member of the oil-rich and garden-friendly Bixby family that owned Rancho Los Alamitos, Susanna started a native plant garden in 1927 on her rancho in Yorba Linda. Later, this garden moved to Claremont College in the foothills of the San Gabriel mountains, about thirty-five miles east of Los Angeles, and became Rancho Santa Ana Botanic Garden.

The 86-acre garden is divided into three distinct areas: Indian Hill Mesa, the East Alluvial Gardens, and the Plant Communities.

It's a wonderful place to wander—lots of local residents use the asphalt paths for daily exercise—but if you're a serious gardener or plant lover, I'd recommend that you arrange to be part of a tour.

Visitors enter the garden on Indian Hill Mesa, a flat-topped hill that's home to the California Courtyard and the California Natives Container Garden. These popular display areas are set up as examples of how native plants can be incorporated into home landscaping. You may be surprised at how interesting and beautiful an environment-friendly native plant garden can be. Using native plants reduces watering (they've adapted themselves to the dry summers) and provides habitat for birds and wildlife. The water issue is making more and more Californians rethink the plants they use in their home landscaping, and Rancho Santa Ana is one place they come to be inspired. The California Cultivar Garden on the north end of the mesa is planted with mature cultivars of native species like California lilacs (*Ceanothus*), cottonwoods, redwoods, and manzanitas.

The East Alluvial Gardens, named for the dense alluvial soils they contain, are located at the base of the eastern edge of the mesa. Here you'll find the Desert Garden and the Coastal Dune and California Channel Islands collections. Two noteworthy Channel Islanders are Catalina ironwood (*Lyonothamnus floribundus*) with red scruffy bark and the aptly named Catalina perfume (*Ribes viburnifolium*), whose crushed leaves give off a sweet, citrusy scent. Here you can visit a long-vanished Tongva village site and see the plants they harvested and used for basketry, home-building, food, and ceremonial purposes. Before you leave the East Alluvial Gardens, pay a visit to the Majestic Oak, estimated to be as much as 250 years old. The trunk and canopy on this native, the oldest resident in the garden, is truly regal.

There are more oaks—dozens of different kinds, including coast live oaks—in the 55-acre Plant Communities section that forms the northern end of Rancho Santa Ana. Here's your opportunity to get off the main paths and explore this remarkable garden in more detail. Brightly colored portals frame the entrances to trails that wind into different parts of Plant Communities. This part of Rancho Santa Ana looks like a wild or natural California landscape, but it's actually a carefully curated and catalogued spectrum of plants from the entire botanical collection.

Throughout Plant Communities, you'll find impressive specimens of wild-collected plants and trees that you would never

The Majestic Oak, a native California oak thought to be 200 to 250 years old, resides in the East Alluvial Gardens at Rancho Santa Ana Botanic Garden.

otherwise see growing together in such close proximity. There's a large, peaceful grove of fourleaf (or four-needled) pinyon pines (*Pinus quadrifolia*) that grow only in southernmost California and northern Baja Mexico. One of my favorite natives in this area is California flannelbush (*Fremontodendron californicum*), a medium-sized evergreen shrub covered with yellow blossoms in the spring; the genus honors Captain John C. Fremont, a nineteenth-century military man and amateur botanist who led four expeditions to the American West in the 1840s. I'm also fond of the oddball boojum trees (*Fouquieria columnaris*) from the desert regions of Baja. These tall, strangely shaped trees got their common name from English botanist Godfrey Sykes who, having seen them in the wild in 1922, was immediately reminded of the mythical Boojums in Lewis Carroll's "The Hunting of the Snark" (nowadays, more people associate the boojum tree with Dr. Seuss's fanciful illustrations than Lewis Carroll's epic nonsense poem). Another desert inhabitant with a somewhat surreal appearance is the Joshua tree (*Yucca brevifolia*), found here at the westernmost part of its range. The Washington fan palm (*Washingtonia robusta*), recognizable by the collapsed layers of dry fronds below its crown, is California's only native palm tree (yes, every other palm tree you see in California is an introduction).

Wonderful scents float through the gardens throughout the year. Smelling the pungent leaves of California bay laurel (*Umbellularia californica*) can give you a temporary brain freeze. California sage (*Artemisia californica*) and jojoba (*Simmondsia chinensis*) are also fragrant delights. If all these California natives have inspired you, go native yourself. The Grow Native plant nursery is near the garden entrance.

The Hortense Miller Garden overlooks
the Pacific Ocean at Laguna Beach.

south coast

california scenario

611 Anton Boulevard, Costa Mesa, CA 92626
southcoastplaza.com/visit/attraction/isamu-noguchis-
    california-scenario/
Visit year-round

- ⏰ Open daily 8am–midnight
- $ Admission free; paid parking in front of location
- 🐕 No dogs

Urban sculpture garden designed by famed artist and landscape architect Isamu Noguchi

It may not be your idea of a "garden" per se, but this unique sculpture park—enclosed by office towers and not visible from the street—distills California's distinctive landforms into an artistic vision that exudes the wonder and repose found in a great garden or landscape. Ironically, or perhaps appropriately, this meditation on the natural world sits in the middle of a manmade environment that is the epitome of corporate sterility.

California Scenario, known locally as the Noguchi Garden, is a public art work installed in 1982 by the great Japanese-American artist Isamu Noguchi (1904–1988). It was commissioned in 1979 by Henry Segerstrom, a wealthy developer whose family had farmed the land that Segerstrom transformed in 1970 into Orange County's most upscale shopping mall. Segerstrom asked Noguchi if he would be interested in creating a sculpture for a garden area between two office towers (called South Coast Plaza) that he was building adjacent to the South Coast mall. Noguchi, by then a world-famous sculptor, furniture designer, and landscape architect, said he would be interested—but only if he could

Isamu Noguchi's California Scenario is a landscape garden created in a plaza between two corporate high-rises.

design the entire garden. And that is what he did. This marvel of
an art garden is open to the public, but it is well-hidden and a bit
tricky to find. Look for the address in front of a long, black building with a double row of palm trees, and pull into the parking
lot. Inside, pass through the building's white marble foyer to the
glass doors at the end of the lobby. When you step outside, you'll
hear the quiet murmur of water and be in the Noguchi Garden.
It's enclosed on two sides by the black, reflective glass walls of the
towers and on the other two sides by tall, adobe-colored walls.

Although primarily known as a sculptor, Noguchi had long been interested in creating public spaces and public art works. With California Scenario, he used his skills as a landscape architect and a sculptor to create an environment that is both minimalist and magnanimous. It uses angular forms, organic shapes, water features, and planted areas to convey the essential components found in California's diverse landscapes. But Noguchi was an artist of wide-ranging talents and styles, and parts of

Noguchi's Spirit of the Lima Bean sculpture commemorates the food crop that was farmed on the land where the garden now stands.

California Scenario may also remind you of cubist or constructivist sculptures.

Noguchi created six scenarios to typify California's aboriginal topography: "Forest Walk," "Land Use," "Desert Land," "Water Source," "Water Use," and "Energy Fountain."

"Forest Walk," to your right as you enter, is an inclined meadow of brilliant green grass with redwoods at the top. The bench up there is a perfect spot to sit and contemplate the other scenarios. Another green and tree-shaded area to your left is "Land Use." Between these two areas is the plaza's pièce de résistance, Noguchi's *Spirit of the Lima Bean*. Noguchi had become known for his interlocking metal sculptures; this one was created with fifteen pieces of caramel-colored granite fitted together like an organic Rubik's cube. Why commemorate the humble lima bean? Because that was the crop Henry Segerstrom's family farmed on the land he turned into South Coast Plaza.

The rest of the plaza is paved with great slabs of sandstone that throw off a hot, desertlike glare or turn cool with shadow, depending on the season and time of day. A shallow, sparkling stream ("Water Source") cuts through the pavement, enlivening the arid scene. "Desert Land," on the other side of the stream, is a mounded oval planted with cacti. "Water Use" is reminiscent of a flume or an irrigation channel. "Energy Fountain" is a towering water chute shaped like a scalene triangle and attached to the rear wall; water courses down a channel in the center.

However you view it—as a giant outdoor installation, a one-man sculpture park, a piece of earth art, or a delightful respite from the autocentric narcissism of Southern California—California Scenario has the timeless elegance and pared-down simplicity of a Japanese landscape painting or Zen garden. Noguchi was also known as a designer for the stage, and when you sit on a bench and contemplate California Scenario, it does look something like a huge stage set. But it's a stage used by real people—primarily office workers taking a break from their cubicles and computer screens in those giant black office blocks. How lucky they are to be able to walk into a piece of art that is also a garden.

You can enjoy this unique urban garden in as little as fifteen minutes. With some advance planning, you could combine it with a visit to the Sherman Library and Gardens in Corona del Mar, the Hortense Miller Garden in Laguna Beach, or Rancho Los Alamitos in Long Beach.

hortense miller garden

Laguna Beach, CA 92652; address available with reservation
hortensemillergarden.org
Visit year-round; February–April for flowering shrubs and trees

....

- 📞 No phone for reservations; tours must be requested through website
- 🕐 Open Tues–Sat 9:45am–noon by advance reservation only
- $ Admission by donation
- ♿ Steep, hilly terrain with narrow paths unsuitable for wheelchairs and those with limited mobility
- 🐕 No dogs

Noteworthy midcentury modern house and garden perched on the crest of a canyon overlooking the Pacific

The places where we create our gardens are the places where we create our lives. Hortense Miller created her garden on the southern slope of Boat Canyon, a deep coastal cleft slightly inland from the Pacific Ocean near Laguna Beach, about forty-four miles southwest of Los Angeles. When she moved in, in 1959, Hortense was fifty years old and the canyon was covered with coastal sage scrub. It still is, except for the remarkable 2.5-acre garden that she spent the rest of her life creating.

But don't come here expecting perfectly manicured beds of brightly colored annuals. That's not what this garden is about. There are many fine and beautiful plants—over 1,500 of them— but they complement rather than dominate the larger landscape. This is an artist's garden, intensely personal but also wonderfully

The midcentury modern home of Hortense Miller is surrounded by gardens filled with drought-tolerant native plants.

A former art student in Chicago, Hortense Miller unleashed her creative energies throughout her house and gardens.

personable, and it naturally makes you wonder about the woman who created it.

First things first, though. Make a reservation a couple of weeks in advance or you won't get in. Hortense left her house and garden to the city of Laguna Beach for use as a public space. The neighbors weren't thrilled with the prospect of visitors driving up their private road to reach the garden, so a gate was installed at the bottom of the street. Once you've arranged for a tour, a docent will meet you, open the gate, and lead you up to the entrance for your tour.

From the road, you can't see the house or garden, only a tangle of sunny roses (*Rosa* 'Mermaid') with bright yellow centers climbing along the boundary fence. A steep, winding path—Hortense laid out all the pathways herself, following the contours of the land—leads down to the house. Along the way it passes a big black locust tree (*Robinia* 'Purple Robe') with showy purple blossoms in the spring. Maybe this tree reminded Hortense of St. Louis, Missouri, where she was born in 1908, and where black locusts were common street trees. They're certainly not common in Laguna Beach.

As you descend the path, the flat-roofed, one-story, midcentury modern house comes into view. Designed by Knowlton Fernald, Jr., the 1,900-square-foot house was meant to be a retirement home for Hortense and her husband, Oscar Miller, a wealthy, much-older Chicago lawyer. Oscar died just three months after they moved in. It was at that point that Hortense began to garden. At first she limited herself to the area immediately around the house, but over the ensuing decades she expanded her reach until the garden covered all 2.5 acres. Along the way, she had help from landscape architect Fred Lang. The plants she chose are predominantly California natives and plants adapted to a Mediterranean climate with low rainfall. Some of the first trees she put in were drought-tolerant Canary Island pines (*Pinus canariensis*).

Hortense created three garden areas. The Wild Garden, planted along a trail on the eastern side of the property, extends to the low-growing coastal sage scrub that dominates the canyon. Among the California native plants in this area, the most beautiful is the fuchsia-flowering gooseberry (*Ribes speciosum*), a drought-tolerant, semi-deciduous plant with glossy green leaves, dense clusters of tubular red flowers in early spring, and too many thorns for comfort. Other drought-tolerant natives found here include buckwheat, artemisia, ceanothus (aka California lilac), sages, and three hardy shrubs with delicate-looking flowers: pink-flowered bush mallow (*Malacothamnus fasciculatus*), yellow bush monkey flower (*Mimulus aurantiacus*), and California rose (*Rosa californica*). Visit earlier in the spring if you want to see these native beauties in flower, as well as Australian natives like weeping bottlebrush (*Callistemon viminalis*).

The courtyard entrance area behind the house is graced by a purple-flowered jacaranda tree and looks up a rise planted with intensely green Korean zoysia grass extending to a handmade tiled wall that serves as a backdrop for special events. The trellis- and house-shaded beds in this area are planted with hybrid camellias, potted begonias, ligularias, and white-flowered evergreen azaleas (*Rhododendron rutherfordiana* 'Alaska'). The large outdoor birdcage housed Hortense's white cockatoo, Dody. During the day, Dody was allowed to fly free and often ended up on the flat, tar-covered roof. Hortense would climb up a ladder to fetch her. She was climbing ladders into her eighties.

A long brick wall inset with small glass bricks conceals an open-air potting shed that's simple, practical, and enjoys a casually stunning view of the shimmering Pacific. Behind it, with the same view, is the Perennial Garden with more California natives and Mediterranean plants. The Catalina cherry tree (*Prunus ilicifolia*), native to the Channel Islands, puts out big clusters of white flowers. Its dazzling companion, a pink cloud cherry (*Prunus serrulata* 'Pink Cloud'), is entirely covered with pink flowers in the spring. Seen against the blue backdrop of the Pacific, the effect is pretty amazing. One of my favorite plants in this area is Scotsman's purse mallow, so called because its yellow purselike flowers never open.

Below the Perennial Garden is the Gazebo Garden, planted with nandina, Japanese crested iris, black mondo grass, clumping bamboos, and a cork oak tree (*Quercus suber*) native to Portugal. Hortense made the elegant, Japanese-style bamboo fence herself. It kept out plant-eating deer and the herd of mountain goats that appeared in Boat Canyon twice a year. Every other wild creature was welcome to visit.

Hortense was a writer and an artist—she studied at the Art Institute of Chicago—and her house is a reflection of her artistic talents and wide-ranging interests. The large and rather startling mural she painted on a wall separating the potting shed from the entrance to the house has the bold imagery of a piece by Georgia O'Keeffe or Frida Kahlo. Hortense was obviously inspired by nature and the natural world. Her home seems to float out over the canyon she called home. She was something of a pioneer, in that she gardened entirely without pesticides and with the intuitive touch of an artist. When she was asked about the informal style of her garden, Hortense said, "This is my garden, not Louis the Fourteenth's. I don't boss this garden, I merely put plants in the ground and let them do as they wish." In the latter part of her life, Hortense did as she wished, too, and this remarkable garden is the happy result.

rancho los alamitos

Historic family ranch with diverse gardens from the 1920s, many designed by the Olmsted Brothers

6400 East Bixby Hill Road, Long Beach, CA 90815
rancholosalamitos.com
Visit year-round; January–March for flowering cacti,
    February–June for flowering trees and native plants

....

📞 (562) 431-3541
🕐 Gardens open Wed–Sun 1–5pm; house accessible only
    via docent-led tour arranged in advance
$ Admission free
🚌 Public transportation
🐾 No dogs

The Secret Garden, adjacent to the house at Rancho Los Alamitos, was a favorite place for Florence Bixby and her grandchildren.

If you like to visit great house-and-garden estates, put Rancho Los Alamitos (Ranch of the Little Cottonwoods) on your must-see list. This remarkable 7.5-acre property, tucked into an upscale gated community in Long Beach (about thirty miles south of Los Angeles), has a charm, authenticity, and historic reach that makes it truly unique. Before you visit, make sure you arrange for a docent-led tour because that's the only way you can step into the ranch house that is essential to the story of Rancho Los Alamitos and its gardens.

That story extends back some 1,500 years, to when this rise of land watered by natural springs was home to the native Tongva people who settled the Los Angeles Basin. In 1790, the Spanish monarchy awarded 300,000 acres of what was coastal sage scrub and chaparral to Manuel Nieto, who'd been part of a Spanish expedition into Alta California. The land grant shrank and changed hands when Mexico ceded what became the state of California to the United States in 1848. In 1878, John and Susan Bixby leased and later purchased the ranch and began a transformation of the house and property that came to a final flowering with their son and daughter-in-law, Fred and Florence Bixby. The Bixbys became a prominent Southern California family in the late nineteenth and early twentieth centuries. Their wealth came from their land and from the Signal Hill oil strike of 1921. It was money from black gold that allowed Florence Bixby to create the remarkable and remarkably preserved gardens that are so enjoyable today. To help her, she enlisted the talents of local garden designers and, in the 1920s, the noted landscape architectural firm Olmsted Brothers of Brookline, Massachusetts.

Over time, eleven different gardens were added, like outdoor rooms around the adobe-core ranch house. The gardens served as a green, shady, colorful buffer zone between the house and the dusty workings of the ranch, which included adjacent livestock barns, fields for crops, and ever-encroaching urban development.

The ranch house is a good place to start your tour, but stop in at the new visitor center first. The center ingeniously incorporates the old horse barn and provides a wealth of interpretive material. Your docent will lead you through the meticulously restored ranch house, built in 1804 as an adobe bunkhouse and altered and enlarged by each successive owner. Filled with original furnishings, the house instantly evokes the comfortable lifestyle and well-to-do tastes of the Bixby family. You enter the house from the Back Patio, designed in 1921 by Paul Howard and notable for its ponytail or elephant's foot palms (*Beaucarnea recurvata*), so called because of the way their trunks bulge at the base. Slip into the white-walled Secret Garden, a charming enclosed garden attached to the southwest corner of the house. It was designed by Olmsted Brothers and used by Florence Bixby as a quiet retreat and a safe haven for her grandchildren. Except for the fine California pepper tree (*Schinus molle*), planted by Susan Bixby long before the Secret Garden was built, all the original plants have been replaced. Despite the name, California pepper trees are natives of Peru and were brought to Mexico and Southern California by the Mission padres.

Head around back, past the sunny South Garden that runs along the length of the south wing. Planted with a border of daylilies, climbing vines, and a gardenia that sent a sweet scent up to Florence Bixby's bedroom, this is a carefree, low-maintenance garden. Continuing south across South Drive, you'll come to the Geranium Walk and Gazebo designed in 1922 by noted Pasadena-based landscape architect Florence Yoch. (In addition to designing real gardens, Yoch designed gardens for movies, including the grounds of Tara in *Gone with the Wind*.) The uphill side of the Geranium Walk is lined with old pepper trees underplanted with blue periwinkle (*Vinca minor*) and graced by an Italian Della Robbia–style plaque. When it was first constructed, this overlook garden offered views all the way to the Pacific. A sweet-smelling reminder of a bygone age and its favorite flowers, the formal Rose Garden on the west end of the Geranium Walk was designed in 1922 by Olmsted Brothers. Both pre-1930 hybrid teas and several varieties of tea roses introduced in Southern California before 1910 are planted within boxwood borders. A replica of Florence

Urns frame the entrance to a cypress allée at Rancho Los Alamitos

Bixby's sundial is set within the Rose Garden's wide brick pathway. At its south end, the Rose Garden opens into the Oleander Walk, another Olmsted Brothers design from 1927. Today, however, this garden is oleanderless and should probably be renamed the Crape Myrtle Walk. The original oleanders planted to screen out unsightly oil wells succumbed to oleander leaf scorch disease in 2001. New oleanders were planted but died of the same blight within three years. They were replaced by crape myrtles, chosen for their colorful pink blossoms and arching habit.

The trimmed cypress hedges surrounding the Olmsted-designed Cypress Steps and Patio originally served as a green backdrop to an eighteenth-century Italian sculpture. Steps lead down into the Cutting Garden, a small, formal, Italianate space anchored by a cistern with a cut metal disk inside, used to hold the heads of cut flowers above the water. The mixed beds are filled with familiar annuals, perennials, and flowering shrubs, including daisies, foxgloves, carnations, dahlias, mums, and hydrangeas.

In 1934, the Olmsteds redesigned the Old Seventh Street Drive as a formal entrance curving up from the front gates to the ranch house. Just north of it, at the south end of the tennis court, you'll find the Friendly Garden. This rectangular garden surrounded by a trellis was used by Florence Bixby to collect and grow cuttings and seeds given to her as gifts from friends. Running along the east side of the tennis court is the Jacaranda Walk, another 1927 Olmsted Brothers design. Blue was Florence Bixby's favorite color and there's plenty of it in this garden: blue jacarandas, purple-blue wisteria, and blue urns that frame the entrance.

Continue north into the striking Cactus Garden, laid out by William Hertrich, the plantsman who created the stunning Desert Garden at the Huntington Library and was superintendent of the gardens there from 1903 to 1948. (The Huntingtons and the Bixbys intermarried.) The Cactus Garden at Rancho Los Alamitos began as an experiment to see if the spineless prickly pear cactus developed by Luther Burbank could be used as cattle fodder (it couldn't) and expanded to include now-giant agaves and other prickly pears. Within it there is a small Shell Garden decorated with abalone and Pismo clam shells, as a memorial to the Bixbys' deceased son.

There are more than native plants in the Native Garden, but the natives—yellow-flowered *Mahonia nevinii*, white-flowered

California buckeye, white and yellow matilija poppies, and bright blue ceanothus—are the most colorful.

The first area to be planted on the estate, two decades before the Bixbys arrived, is the appropriately named Old Garden. A pepper tree there dates from 1845. In 1921, Florence Bixby commissioned Paul Howard, and later the Olmsted Brothers, to design the garden as a boundary screen. Boxwood, clipped cypress, yellow-green banana trees, and bamboo form successive layers of color, texture, and form.

Check out the lovely little Music Patio, scene of small concerts and events, and then head to the Front Lawn to have a look at the enormous Moreton Bay figs (*Ficus macrophylla*). These trees, native to Moreton Bay, Australia, were planted in 1890 by John and Susan Bixby, the fourth owners and the first Bixbys to call Rancho Los Alamitos home. In 1968, their grandchildren donated what was left of the family ranch to the City of Long Beach as a public oasis and a small, valuable and still-vital remnant of Southern California history.

sherman library and gardens

2647 East Pacific Coast Highway, Corona del Mar, CA 92625
slgardens.org
Visit year-round; January–March for cacti and succulent
    blooms

....

- 📞 (949) 673-2261
- 🕐 Gardens open daily 10:30am–4pm; library Mon–Fri
    10:30am–4pm; closed Thanksgiving, Dec 25, Jan 1
- $ Admission by donation
- 🐕 No dogs

Modest but wide-ranging and meticulously tended display garden in upscale beach town

Just south of Newport Beach, the famed Pacific Coast Highway
(Highway 1) passes through the oceanside community of Corona
del Mar. The beach, a crescent of white sand with rocky outcrops
and fluttering palm trees, is undeniably alluring. But for those
whose interests are more botanical than beachy, the Sherman
Library and Gardens is the star attraction in this affluent town. It
fronts Highway 1, Corona del Mar's main drag, but its treasures
are mostly hidden from view by a tasteful cream-colored wall. The
plant collections in this small (2.2 acres) botanic garden are surprisingly wide-ranging and meticulously displayed. Its manageable
size is part of its appeal: you can see everything on a leisurely one-
hour stroll and come away refreshed and maybe inspired.

The story of how this charming garden got off the ground,
or rather *into* the ground, is a tale of wealth, loyalty, and philan-
thropy. It's named for Moses Hazeltine Sherman (1853–1933),
a New Englander who became one of California's wealthiest

The new Succulent
Garden at the
Sherman Library uses
cacti and succulents to
create an otherworldly
gardenscape.

citizens, but it sits on land owned and bequeathed to the Sherman Foundation by Arnold Haskell (1895–1977), Sherman's personal assistant. Moses was in the right place (the Pacific Southwest) at the right time (from the 1870s through the 1930s), investing in all the right stuff: mining, cattle, and California real estate—you've heard of Sherman Oaks?—back when it was still affordable. When Sherman died, Haskell continued to handle his mentor's business interests. In the 1950s, he began buying up property in Corona del Mar; eventually he owned an entire block. A plant lover and bibliophile, he founded Sherman Library and Gardens in 1966 with the goal of turning it into a community center with a notable botanic garden and research library.

The small Sun Garden that you see upon entering changes with the seasons; when I visited, it was planted with grasses and cosmos that waved in the ocean breezes and gave it a meadowlike feel. Follow your nose and check out some of the fragrant plants growing around the perimeter and in nearby beds. Depending on the season, you might be treated to the scents of sweet olive (*Osmanthus fragrans*); sausage vine (*Holboellia coriacea*), a hardy climber related to akebia that produces purple sausagelike fruits; and hyssop (*Agastache*). A small adjacent Rose Garden is festooned with many old-fashioned heirloom varieties and a pretty David Austin scented climber (*Rosa* 'Red Eden Rose'). More good scents emanate from the corner Fruit and Fragrance Garden, where *Gardenia taitensis* and *Hibiscus acetosella* 'Haight Ashbury' are planted among pineapple, starfruit, Thai lime, and guava trees.

Step into the Tropical Conservatory, clad in strips of redwood lath, to have a look at the notable orchid collection, several varieties of anthuriums, bananas, and colorful lobster claws (*Heliconia rostrata*), their pinkish red flowers edged with yellow. Flanking the western corners of the conservatory are a Carnivorous Bog Garden (don't worry, only flies are trapped and digested by the endangered pitcher plants, *Nepenthes*) and a rich collection of bromeliads.

There's a film noir quality to the light in the conservatory and adjacent Shade House, where the bright Corona del Mar sun casts strong bars of shadow through the lath and latticework. In the

The Sherman Library in Corona del Mar is home to one of the largest begonia collections in Southern California.

Specimen Shade Garden located in the Shade House, have a look at the impressive begonia collection. Dozens of unusual begonias, including palm leaf begonia (*Begonia luxurians*), cane begonia, and a rare scented variety, occupy an entire wall. It's among the best potted begonia collections I've ever encountered (the other is at the Mendocino Coast Botanical Gardens).

The nearby Perennial Shade Garden is home to shade-loving beauties like the Australian tree fern (*Cyathea cooperi*), baby queen palm (*Chamaedorea plumosa*), black mondo grass (*Ophiopogon planiscapus* 'Nigrescens'), and Japanese maples (*Acer palmatum*). There are intriguing details and eye-catching colors, shapes, and textures everywhere you look in this garden. You'll see stairs with sedums growing in the risers and a fountain dripping with succulents instead of water. Specimen trees abound. The palm collection includes straight-trunked queen palms (*Syagrus romanzoffiana*) from South America; a traveler's palm (*Ravenala madagascariensis*) that's not really a palm (it's more closely related to strelitzia, or bird of paradise) but looks like one, with enormous paddle-shaped leaves; a needle palm (*Rhapidophyllum hystrix*), a super-hardy subtropical palm from the southern United States that takes temperatures of -20 degrees Fahrenheit (you could almost grow it in Minnesota); and a triangle palm (*Dypsis decaryi*), an endangered native of Madagascar, with leaves that grow almost directly from the trunk and arch gracefully outward.

Don't miss the new Succulent Garden located next to the breezy and elegant Patio Restaurant (reserve in advance for brunch or lunch). Designed by Matt Maggio, this theatrical little tour de force features an amazing palette of aloes, cacti, and dramatically shaped specimen trees planted on and against a stage set of bright white rocks that give it the look of an underwater coral reef. It's too well done to be called whimsical, and you'll find yourself marveling at the colors and shapes of the plants individually and as an ensemble.

Before you leave, pay a visit to the small 1940s-era adobe house that was on this Corona del Mar property when Arnold Haskell bought it in the 1950s, then have a quick look at the charming interior of the Sherman Library itself. This building, which once served as Haskell's business office, is devoted to the history of the Pacific Southwest, where Moses Sherman made his fortune. These are the people behind the plants that grace the remarkable gardens just outside.

south coast botanic garden

26300 Crenshaw Boulevard, Palos Verdes, CA 90274
southcoastbotanicgarden.org
Visit year-round; December–February for cactus; April–June
for flowering fruit trees and California native plants;
midsummer to late fall for dahlias

- ☎ (310) 544-1948
- ⏰ Open daily 9am–5pm; closed Dec 25
- $ Admission fee
- 🐕 No dogs

A pioneering reclamation project
that now boasts scores of botanical
treasures atop a former landfill

South Coast Botanic Garden is home to an official All-America Rose Selections garden that features more than 1,600 roses.

As you explore the colorful delights of this 87-acre botanical garden, you might be walking atop your grandmother's old Kelvinator Foodarama fridge, or the worn-out tires of a 1958 Edsel. Why is that? Because what is today the South Coast Botanic Garden was used until 1961 as a landfill for Los Angeles County. And before that, it was an open-pit mine. Part of what makes this garden so unique is that it was one of world's first land reclamation projects. It has served as a model for similar projects the world over. Even Prince Charles, who's ahead of the curve when it comes to environmental issues, has visited South Coast. There's no hint of that landfill today, nor of the mining operations that preceded it. Birds and butterflies flit amid the flowering trees and shrubs, and 100,000 visitors a year stop by to stroll and admire the plant collections.

A few million years ago, the Palos Verdes Peninsula where the garden is located (ten miles south of Los Angeles airport) was entirely underwater. When the oceans receded, a sediment of diatomaceous earth was left behind—useful to humans as an aerating and binding agent in cement. So, at the turn of the twentieth century, the chalky deposits of long-dead diatoms began to be mined. The mining operations grew until some 200 acres were a vast open-pit mine. In 1956, when the resource was depleted, the mining company sold the land to Los Angeles County. That's when it became a sanitary landfill. In the early 1960s, the landfill was capped and local citizens and conservation groups managed to get eighty-seven of the 200 acres designated as a botanical garden. The first plantings—40,000 trees—arrived in 1961, and the garden opened to the public in 1965. Today this reclaimed land is home to about 200,000 plants.

For a look at the highlights, follow the one-mile Tram Road loop that winds around the periphery of the garden. The road is bisected by many smaller paths that lead to nooks and crannies within the garden. Give yourself at least an hour. You might want to enjoy a picnic lunch while you're here. The garden is a year-round hive of activity, from plant demonstration classes to evening concerts.

Several smaller gardens are clustered around the entrance. The Japanese(-style) Garden with a koi pond, evergreen shrubs, and 200-year-old lanterns made of Okazaki stone is a calm spot. Near it, shaded from the hot California sun, is the Fuchsia Garden. Maintained by the South Coast branch of the National Fuchsia

Society, this is the only fuchsia collection of its kind in L.A. County and contains many different species and cultivars. You'll also find in this area the Dahlia Garden, adding much-needed color from midsummer to late fall; the ever-changing Volunteer Flower Garden, a kind of pet flower garden tended by South Coast volunteers; and the Vegetable Garden.

The first real highlight, the Desert Garden, is close by. You can't miss it. Growing within a rocky, bone-dry desertscape are cacti, agaves, and succulents. Although it's laid out according to region, with prickly pears (*Opuntia*) in one area and pincushion cacti (*Mammillaria*) in another, this is in no way the kind of heavily groomed and artistically arranged cactus garden that you'd find at the Huntington Library in San Marino. (Actually, that's part of what makes South Coast so appealing.) January and February are the best times to visit the Desert Garden, when you can enjoy a surprising array of cactus blossoms, from the gorgeous purple flowers of the rose cactus (*Pereskia grandifolia*) to the yellow blossoms on the prickly pears and the bright red-orange flames of the ocotillos (*Fouquieria splendens*).

If you prefer thorns on rose bushes rather than cacti, head north on Tram Road to the 11.5-acre Rose Garden. Started in 1990 and renovated in 2015, this All-America Rose Selections garden dazzles the eyes and nose with over 1,600 roses, including hybrids, teas, grandifloras, floribundas, and David Austin English roses; the top AARS winners have a one-acre winner's circle all to themselves.

Stop by the touchy-feely Garden of the Senses to stroke a few plants and inhale some marvelous scents, then head up to the Mediterranean Garden. Here you'll find drought-tolerant plants unique to the five regions of the world that have hot, dry summers and mild, rainy winters: coastal California and Chile, the Mediterranean Basin, southwest Australia, and the southwest Cape of South Africa.

You'll find about twenty different taxa in the Ficus Collection, but the stars are the Moreton Bay figs (*Ficus macrophylla*),

Once a landfill, South Coast Botanic Garden is now full of colorful specimen plants like this red hot poker, *Kniphofia hirsuta* 'Fire Dance'.

whose huge twisted roots dangle from branches and creep along the ground. It's about ten degrees cooler in the banyan grove, and the grove is underplanted with bright orange clivias. Other residents include *F. petiolaris* from Mexico, with pinkish red–veined leaves, and the wide-spreading sycamore fig (*F. sycomorus*), cultivated since ancient times in Egypt and the Mideast. The white fig (*F. virens*), native to southeast Asia and northern Australia, is one of the ominous "strangler figs" that can germinate and grow in other trees, slowly strangling its host.

Continuing east on Tram Road you'll come next to a modest Palm Collection. It mostly consists of fan palms but also contains Chilean wine palms, whose sap was harvested for wine (so much so that the tree is nearly extinct in the wild); the cold-tolerant blue hesper palm (*Brahea armata*), with waxy stems, silvery blue fronds, and fragrant white flowers; and the ponytail palm (*Beaucarnea recurvata*) that isn't a true palm but grows long palmlike fronds.

As you stroll along the Tram Road loop you'll come to the Ginkgo Grove, the Rare Fruit Orchard, the Eucalyptus/Myrtaceae Collection with eucalyptus trees (love those sweet-smelling lemon gums) and brachychitons (as in bottle trees, a plant that's

estimated to be 50 million years old). Then you'll come to the California Native Plants section. More and more California gardeners and landscapers are waking up to the fact that using natives like the ones found here (and in the Mediterranean Garden) is beneficial to the environment in many ways. The plants are drought-tolerant and provide much-needed habitat and food for birds, butterflies, bees, and other wildlife. And they're beautiful—visit in the spring and you'll see.

There's much more to discover at South Coast Botanic Garden than I have room to describe here. And the horde of botanical treasures you'll find aboveground today have their roots in—of all things—the discarded detritus of yesteryear.

The unearthly blue pool in the Aloë Garden at Lotusland in Montecito.

santa barbara & vicinity

alice keck park memorial gardens

1500 Santa Barbara Street, Santa Barbara, CA 93102
santabarbaraca.gov
Visit year-round

- 📞 (805) 897-1917
- $ Admission free
- 🐕 Dogs on leash

A large landscaped park that is both old-fashioned and up-to-date, in the heart of Santa Barbara

Mexican fan palms and a gazebo overlook a pond filled with koi and turtles at Alice Keck Park Memorial Gardens.

Alice Keck was a Park who had a park named after her. The park naming didn't happen until after her death in 1977, because she wanted her gift of one city block to the city of Santa Barbara to remain anonymous during her lifetime. Before she married a Park, Alice was a Keck—the daughter of William Myron Keck, founder of Superior Oil Company. And today, the park that was named for her is affectionately known as "Alice."

Wandering through this pleasant five-acre city park, it's difficult to imagine the kinds of real estate wars and zoning battles that preceded it. Mrs. Park's park is a rare happy ending to a story that could have had a very different outcome—and probably would have, if the residents of Santa Barbara hadn't banded together to protect their low-rise city from high-rise condo development.

People often think public parks are "just there," but in fact creating a park is typically a long, difficult, and often contentious process, especially when the land is worth as much as it is in Santa Barbara. The city was platted into square blocks back in 1853. The city council back then decreed that sixteen blocks—including this one—were to be used as public plazas. Predictably, as the city grew, that decree gave way to development, and by 1893, all but a couple of those blocks had been sold.

In 1904, the block that is now Alice was sold to Mary Miles Herter, a wealthy widow whose husband had been a founder of Herter Brothers, a famous New York design firm. Mary Miles Herter was a Gilded Age New Yorker who came West to revel in the sunny climes of Santa Barbara. The so-called bungalow she had built as the family's Santa Barbara digs was so enormous that her son, Albert, and his wife Adele (both artists and designers) eventually turned it into the ultra-posh El Mirasol Hotel. Every year, the J. P. Morgans, the Vanderbilts, the Crockers, the Rockefellers, the Guggenheims, the Armours, and the Kennedys would roll into Santa Barbara on their private rail cars and spend a month or two in the spacious private bungalows nestled amid El Mirasol's lavish gardens.

The Gilded Age became the Golden Age (in Hollywood, anyway), and then Old Age, as El Mirasol sank into decrepitude and neglect. Eventually, after a couple of fires, it was demolished in the 1960s.

Enter The Developers. The first plan to erect a nine-story condo tower on the site was nixed by neighbors. The second plan for two eleven-story towers with an arts center thrown in to sweeten the deal met a similar fate. The battles went on for years until an anonymous donor bought the property and donated it to Santa Barbara for use as a public park. That donor was Alice Keck Park (1918–1977). Little is known about her except that she suffered from attacks of paranoia, traveled a lot in Europe, and eventually returned to live in Santa Barbara. She had a distant connection to the El Mirasol site because her aunt Caroline had been married to Albert and Adele Herter's son, Everit, who died in World War I.

Alice (the person) wanted the Santa Barbara Botanic Garden to develop and oversee the landscaping of Alice (the park). To that end, Elizabeth Kellam de Forest was asked to be supervising landscape architect. Elizabeth and her late husband, the landscape architect Lockwood de Forest, Jr., had been trendsetting garden designers in Santa Barbara since the 1920s and active in the Santa Barbara Botanic Garden for decades. Elizabeth de Forest chose Grant Castleberg as the landscape designer. The design Castleberg produced turned Alice into Santa Barbara's most appealing public park, a wonderful place to stroll, relax, and observe nature. The fronds of tall Mexican fan palms gleam and flutter high overhead. Along the winding paths, you'll encounter rustic features like a small bridge that spans a gurgling stream, and a gazebo that overlooks a pond filled with koi and turtles. Bougainvillea cascades over sandstone perimeter walls, providing brilliant splashes of color, and a variety of xeriscape plants have been added to help reduce water usage. It's a park that's both a step back in time, in the best sense, and contemporary. Thanks to Alice Keck Park (and the residents of Santa Barbara), the park that bears her name fits beautifully into a fine old neighborhood. Instead of more concrete and glass, it provides Santa Barbara with green, growing life.

When they open, the scarlet flowers of fireman's cap (*Erythrina* ×*bidwillii*) provide a brilliant contrast to lime-green asparagus ferns at Alice Keck Park Memorial Gardens.

casa del herrero

1387 East Valley Road, Montecito, CA 93108
casadelherrero.com
Visit year-round

....

- 📞 (805) 565-5653 ext. 202 (reservations)
- 🕐 Open mid-February–mid-November Wed and Sat by advance reservation and on docent-led tour only (no children under 10); 90-minute tours at 10am and 2pm
- $ Admission fee
- 🐕 No dogs

Antiques-filled Spanish Colonial Revival home and gardens from the 1920s and 1930s

Two fascinating and unforgettable garden estates in the wealthy enclave of Montecito should be at the top of your list of must-see sights in Santa Barbara County. Casa del Herrero is one, Lotusland is the other. With some planning, you can visit both of these extraordinary places on the same day, but you need to reserve your tours well in advance. These are not general admission gardens, where you can wander in and around at will; docent-led tours are the only way you can see them.

Casa del Herrero (House of the Blacksmith) is a superb example of a house and garden built during the heyday of the Country Place Era of the 1920s and 1930s. That was when a host of wealthy Americans discovered the Mediterranean-like charms of California and built grand houses adorned with lavish gardens. Though Spanish Colonial homes and ornamental gardens were hardly new features in the California landscape, the Country Place Era codified that historic style, enlarged it, and combined it with other European styles. Casa del Herrero so perfectly reflects this aesthetic—and has been so little altered since it was built, over ninety years ago—that it's been designated a National Historic Landmark.

A bedroom window at Casa del Herrero overlooks the long, descending axis of the gardens.

The 11-acre estate was the home and workshop of an industri-
alist and engineer named George Fox Steedman (1873–1940) and
his wife, Carrie. Back in his hometown of St. Louis, George and
his two brothers purchased a foundry, Curtis & Co., and turned
it into a commercial success. Profits skyrocketed when George
gained a game-changing contract with the British government to
manufacture and supply "projectile ammunition" to Allied troops
in World War I. In 1921, he and Carrie traveled to Santa Barbara
to visit George's ailing brother and fell in love with the climate,
the colors, and the relaxed ambience. A take-charge kind of guy,
George purchased land in Montecito Valley in 1923 and assem-
bled an A-list team of architects, landscape architects, and interior
designers to create his new California country place. The house
was nearing completion when, in 1925, a disastrous earthquake
struck, reducing downtown Santa Barbara to rubble. George

Casa del Herrero epitomizes the glamorous Country Place Era.

made his way out to his new home, expecting to find it destroyed. But there it stood, without so much as a crack. Maybe he thought it was a good omen, because he moved into the house that very day, and in 1930 he and Carrie made Casa del Herrero their permanent residence.

Though garden lovers will want to concentrate on what's outside, the house is an integral part of the Casa del Herrero landscape. George Washington Smith, the main architect, moved to Montecito in 1915 and established himself as a foremost residential architect of the period. Smith is credited with popularizing the Spanish Colonial Revival style reflected in Casa del Herrero and other post-earthquake buildings in downtown Santa Barbara. Casa del Herrero is something of a stage set, though, with a front façade reminiscent of a sober Andalusian palace and a dazzling white back with Italianate touches. The house is all the more remarkable for its collection of sixteenth- and seventeenth-century Spanish antiques, tiles, and furnishings, purchased by Steedman on a trip to Spain in 1923 with New York antiquarians Arthur and Mildred Stapley Byne (they also advised William Randolph Hearst when he was furnishing Hearst Castle). Antiques aside, there's much to admire here, including an octagonal library on the first floor, a graceful curved staircase in the foyer, and an airy second-floor sleeping porch that looks out over palm trees and greenery.

Behind the house, patios and courtyards provide a seamless transition into the captivating gardens. Steedman chose Ralph Stevens, a landscape architect born in Montecito (he was the son of the nurseryman who first purchased the property that became Lotusland), to create the initial garden design. Lockwood de Forest, Jr., the noted landscape architect and designer, was also called in to help. De Forest was a sophisticated Easterner, familiar with the gardens and architecture of Spain and the Mediterranean; Stevens was an expert plant person. The final plan resulted in two main gardens with adjacent areas set aside for a cutting garden, a kitchen garden, and an orchard.

The south garden extends in a long axis from a formal, semi-enclosed courtyard behind the house. This is very much a Moorish-influenced design, embellished with two fountains—a star-shaped one at the top of the garden, a square one at the bottom. The garden between them, enclosed by a closely cropped eugenia hedge, gently descends two levels to a curved terminus with a central opening that leads down one final level to a cactus garden. The long axis features a central strip of lawn with plantings of ferns, begonias, cinnabar lilies, mahonias, and dragon trees (*Dracaena draco*) along the sides. It's all very contained, very formal, very much a complementary component of the house.

The east garden radiates out from the charming Spanish patio with its small fountain. A rectangular planting area with parterres enclosing a French rose garden terminates in a fan-shaped exedra reminiscent of ancient Roman gardens throughout the Mediterranean. Beds close to the patio are planted with an eye-catching array of blue and white flowers. Look, too, for the intriguing dovecote and sundial decorated with signs of the zodiac. In this idyllic setting, Carrie Steedman oversaw the garden while her

The formal structure of the gardens at Casa del Herrero is integral to the Spanish Colonial Revival architecture used throughout.

husband George concentrated on his new passion, silversmithing, along with metal working, photography, and winemaking. His obsessively precise and workaholic nature is reflected in his amazing workshop on the west side of the house. A gem of the Arts and Crafts style, the meticulously ordered workshop is a fascinating museum in its own right. George had forty-four patents by the time he died in 1940 at age sixty-nine. Carrie lived in the house until her death in 1963. The Steedmans' daughter, Medora, and their grandchildren later set up a foundation to preserve the architectural and horticultural legacy of Casa del Herrero. And by the way, why is it named House of the Blacksmith? Because of the ornamental Spanish-style *rejas* (grille) and other wrought-iron work on the façade.

lotusland

695 Ashley Road, Santa Barbara, CA 93108 (mailing address; Montecito entrance address provided with tour reservation)
lotusland.org
Visit when open

....

- 📞 (805) 969-9990 (reservations)
- 🕐 Open only during timed-entry tours, Feb 15–Nov 15
  Wed–Sat 10am and 1:30pm; reservation required
- $ Admission fee
- 🐕 No dogs

World-class garden of a flamboyant opera singer, home to 3,500 different plants

As extravagant as its creator, the Water Garden at Lotusland shimmers with exotic lotuses and waterlilies.

When the gates of Lotusland swing open, you enter a garden world unlike any you've ever seen. For sheer botanical splendor, the only garden in Southern California that can rival it is the Huntington Library in San Marino. But when it comes to garden as theater, garden as glamor, garden as diva, Lotusland stands alone. It's expensive to get in, and you need to reserve well in advance (only 13,500 visitors are allowed per year), but it's worth it because visiting Lotusland is a truly unforgettable experience.

Like a much-married lady, Lotusland has assumed several different names over the past century. Its first name, Tanglewood, was bestowed in 1882 by Ralph Stevens, who set up the 37-acre estate as a home and demonstration nursery. Several palm trees planted during the Tanglewood era thrive to this day. In 1916, new owners Mr. and Mrs. Erastus Palmer Gavit rechristened the estate Cuesta Linda (Pretty Hill). In the 1920s, this New York (via Albany) society couple built a Spanish Colonial Revival home and added the requisite swimming pool. An olive allée and a set of water stairs remain from the Cuesta Linda years. When the Polish opera singer Ganna Walska bought the property in 1941, she renamed it Tibetland on the advice of her sixth husband, a calculating "yogi" twenty years her junior who wanted to create a spiritual retreat for Tibetan monks (and a nice home for himself). But when that scheme fell through, and the yogi tried to divorce her and claim alimony, Walska gave her guru the boot (she had a prenuptial agreement that protected her property) and renamed the estate Lotusland, in honor of the lotus plant sacred to ancient Egyptians and Indians. Ganna, you see, was searching for spiritual enlightenment. After six husbands, what else was there? Gardening, as it turned out.

The creation of Lotusland became the focus of her life for over forty years. She poured into Lotusland all the cash, cachet, and chutzpah that she had accrued during a lifetime of self-invention, self-promotion, and self-improvement. If ever there was a life waiting to be made into a miniseries, it's Ganna Walska's.

Born Hanna Puacz in Poland in 1887, the budding performer aspired to the stage and studied singing, changing her name to the grander-sounding Madame Ganna Walska. At age twenty, she eloped with a Russian count, a marriage that was soon annulled. After moving from Paris to New York to escape World War I, she met a wealthy doctor twice her age who treated her for a throat ailment and married her ten days later. When he died, Ganna turned her sights on the astronomically wealthy heir to the International Harvester fortune. He was inconveniently married, but influential at the Chicago Opera. In 1920, aboard the *Aquitania*, on the way back to France, Ganna met another heir, this one to the Smith Carpet Manufacturing fortune. He proposed two days later and they married. Heir No. 1 then showed up in Paris, freshly divorced, and begged Hanna/Ganna to leave Heir No. 2. Eventually she did divorce him and, three months later, married Heir No. 1. Did that contract he'd secured for her to sing at the Chicago Opera have anything to do with it? The scandal that accompanied this drama wrecked those plans in Chicago, so as a consolation prize, Heir No. 1 purchased the Théâtre des Champs Élyseés in Paris for his beautiful songbird. They divorced because, now having a theater of her own, homes in Paris and New York, and a chateau in the Loire Valley, Ganna wouldn't move to Chicago (would you?). A physicist and inventor became Husband No. 5, but he died after Ganna had fled Europe in 1940 to escape the Nazi occupation of Paris. That brings us to New York, and the yoga instructor who talked her into moving to the more free-spirited land of California, where the beautiful Montecito estate known as Cuesta Linda was for sale. What is so amazing about Ganna's story is that she passed herself off as a singer but she really couldn't sing. Remember that ambitious but untalented opera singer in *Citizen Kane*? Orson Welles reputedly based that character on Ganna Walska.

But enough gossip. Walska's real achievement was Lotusland. The garden is a series of grouped plant collections and theme gardens that show a pronounced theatrical flair and an artist's eye for color, shape, and texture. Ganna had expert help and advice from landscape architects Lockwood de Forest, Jr., and Ralph Stevens (son of the original owner), among others, but I think it's safe to say that the overall vision for Lotusland was hers. A docent will lead you on a ninety-minute tour of the highlights. But be forewarned, Lotusland is home to over 3,500 different kinds of plants

The opera singer Ganna Walska lived in a house she surrounded with cacti and theatrical gardens.

and is so intricately planted and lavishly conceived that it's almost impossible to take in on one visit.

Ganna loved spiky succulents and you'll encounter a lot of them—huge, bold, dramatic—at Lotusland. The Aloe Garden, for example, comprises some 160 taxa of aloes—including giant tree aloes from South Africa, Madagascar, and Yemen— and eighty-five taxa of succulent euphorbias. But because this is Lotusland, you'll also find in with the aloes and euphorbias a fountain made out of giant clamshells and a crescent-shaped pool edged with abalone. The equally outstanding Bromeliad Garden is home to both terrestrial and epiphytic varieties. The pincushion and saguaro cacti in front of the main house were planted in the 1940s, but the Cactus Garden was created in 2001, after Ganna's death, with an extensive assemblage that a collector had promised to her in 1966. Three hundred tons of basalt was used to create the elevated planting beds.

Spikes and spines may have appealed to the prickly side of Ganna's gardening personality, but there was a tender side, too. You'll see it in the amazing Fern Garden with its huge begonias and in the soft, shimmering splendor of the Lotus Garden. Ganna revamped the old swimming pool for this aquatic extravaganza of hardy and tropical waterlilies and exotic lotus plants. Cycads were

The Blue Garden at Lotusland is a dramatic landscape created over a forty-year period.

a relatively late passion in Ganna's horticultural love life, and in 1977 she auctioned off her jewels to pay for a new million-dollar cycad garden. Completed in 1979, it contains over 200 species of these ancient and now extremely endangered plants.

The various theme gardens cover all manner of botanical conceits. For the ethereal Blue Garden, started in 1948, Ganna chose only plants with silvery to blue-gray foliage. A blue Atlas cedar and a grove of 130 rare Chilean wine palms are underplanted with blue fescue and succulent blue chalk sticks (*Senecio mandraliscae*), with Mexican blue palms (*Brahea armata*) as accents. The pathways are lined with blue-green glass slag that Ganna purchased from a local bottling factory. Though the theme gardens are often meant to be reminiscent of opera sets, their theatrical flourishes occasionally verge on decorative overkill. But that, too, is part of Lotusland's overall mise-en-scène.

I don't have space here to detail all the wonders in this wonderland of a garden. Suffice it to say that Ganna Walska gardened like the prima donna she was. She described herself as "the enemy of the average" and lived by the credo that more is better. She never had the operatic career she coveted, but her voice comes through loud and clear in this garden.

santa barbara botanic garden

1212 Mission Canyon Road, Santa Barbara, CA 93105
sbbg.org
Visit in spring, when native wildflowers are in spectacular
bloom

- 📞 (805) 682-4726
- 🕐 Open daily Mar–Oct 9am–6pm, Nov 9am–5pm
- $ Admission fee
- ♿ Modified tour available for wheelchairs (with advance notice)
- 🐕 No dogs

Cacti, perennials, and an extraordinary meadow in a garden dedicated to California's native plants

So many of California's great garden estates epitomize the wonders of gardening in a Mediterranean climate (with a lot of money at your disposal). The Santa Barbara Botanic Garden epitomizes the wonders of California's native plant communities—not only their beauty, but also their hardiness, adaptability, and resilience. If you're a plant lover, plan to spend at least a couple of hours here, and bring your hiking shoes so you can explore the garden's many trails.

The idea of establishing a botanic garden in conjunction with the Santa Barbara Museum of Natural History was put forward by the Carnegie Institute in 1925. The plan took off in 1928 when a local philanthropist named Anna Dorinda Blaksley Barnes Bliss presented thirteen acres of land in Mission Canyon to the museum. That parcel and subsequent additions provide sea-to-mountain views and a variety of landforms and habitats ideally suited to the garden's focus on plants representative of

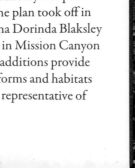

California poppies, lupines, and clarkia are a few of the spring wildflower showstoppers in the Meadow Section of the Santa Barbara Botanic Garden.

the California Floristic Province's four distinct plant zones. The site has historic significance as well. In the early 1800s, Native American laborers from Mission Santa Barbara built a stone dam and wooden aqueduct to carry water from Mission Creek to the Franciscan mission. Today, the garden is a Santa Barbara County Historic Landmark.

Pick up a map at the visitor center and have a look at the information kiosk designed by Lockwood de Forest, Jr., in 1937. From this point you have many options for exploring the 78-acre garden. If you're visiting in the spring, head first to the adjacent 1.5-acre Meadow Section to feast your eyes on the spectacular and justly famous wildflower display. Brilliant orange California

Beware the clawlike thorns of *Agave shawii* at the Santa Barbara Botanic Garden.

poppies, succulent lupines, meadow foam, farewell-to-spring, and other California native wildflowers carpet the site. Later in the season, the Meadow becomes a more subdued mosaic of perennial bunchgrasses and herbs characteristic of California's grasslands. A stand of mature coast live oaks (*Quercus agrifolia*) can be seen along the Meadow's western edge, and a large collection of *Dudleya* species, rare succulent plants found mostly in the coastal regions, is showcased on its eastern side.

To the north, the so-called Indian Steps—thought to be the path taken by the Native Americans who built the dam and aqueduct in 1807—lead down to the floodplain of Mission Creek and a grove of stately coast redwoods (*Sequoia sempervirens*), the oldest specimens planted in 1926. In the spring, the beautiful flowers of California rose bay (*Rhododendron macrophyllum*) and western azalea (*R. occidentale*) brighten this cool, shady woodland scene. A trail in the southwestern corner of the Redwood Section accesses the Campbell Trail and Chaparral Section, devoted to plant communities on the dry, rocky slopes of California's coastal and interior mountain ranges. The deep-rooted, thick-leaved, evergreen shrubs and plants of the chaparral have adapted to wildfires and quickly regenerate in burned areas.

In 2009, the Jesusita wildfire swept through the riparian corridor of Mission Creek and up the surrounding canyon slopes, reducing some areas in the garden's Canyon Section to an ashy moonscape. You can see the rapid and remarkable post-fire regeneration process along sections of Canyon Trail and Creek Trail in the southwest part of the garden, and along the Pritchett Trail in the northwest. Only three weeks after parts of the Pritchett Trail were burned to the ground, tough native plants like toyon, lemonade berry, sycamore, California bay, and scrub oak began to sprout from underground stumps and roots—an adaptation that enables plants in fire-prone areas to recover rapidly and take advantage of increased light and nutrients provided by the ash. The fresh new growth is a heartening reminder of Nature's ability to restore itself. Not everything along Mission Creek was lost in the fire. California bay laurels (*Umbellularia californica*), western sycamores (*Platanus racemosa*), big-leaf maples (*Acer macrophyllum*), white alders (*Alnus rhombifolia*), and coast live oaks still shade the stream and grow alongside it.

As you head back toward the garden entrance and administration buildings, there are four additional areas well worth exploring. The Desert Section is one of the garden's oldest and most prominent features. Here you'll find a large and varied collection of cactus and other species that grow in California's hot, arid coastal and interior deserts. If you visit in the spring or early summer, you'll be treated to an eye-popping display of flowering desert plants, including purple-flowering desert-willow (*Chilopsis linearis*), yellow-flowered palo verde (*Parkinsonia florida*), and the brilliant red-flowering ocotillo (*Fouquieria splendens*). Just south of the Desert Section is the Water Wise Home Garden, where you can be inspired by a landscape of water-conserving California native plants adapted to a variety of home landscape uses.

Manzanitas (*Arctostaphylos*), with their smooth red bark, delicate flower clusters, and sculptural shapes, are widespread throughout California. You'll find sixty of the state's approximately ninety taxa, and dozens of cultivars, in the garden's Manzanita Section. Besides manzanitas, this section also features mature specimens of big-leaf maple (*Acer macrophyllum*), bigcone spruce (*Pseudotsuga macrocarpa*), and gray pine (*Pinus sabiniana*). In the spring, however, all eyes are on the spectacular Canyon Pink California buckeye (*Aesculus californica* 'Canyon Pink'), a showy selection introduced by the garden. Before you go, stroll through the Japanese Teahouse Garden at the bottom of the Arroyo Section. This small, serene garden was designed with all the traditional elements of a Japanese tea garden, but uses only California native plants to create its effects. Manzanitas, madrones, and Port Orford cedars add a sculptural quality to the garden and are combined with low-growing mosses, ferns, and wild strawberry to create a serene and contemplative environment. The teahouse was built in Kyoto in 1949 and donated to the Santa Barbara Botanic Garden in 1998.

Give yourself time to browse in the Garden Growers Nursery, too. I think you can guess what they sell. Yes, California native plants.

The desert-themed gardens at Sunnylands Center and Gardens are a new addition to the Annenberg estate in Rancho Mirage.

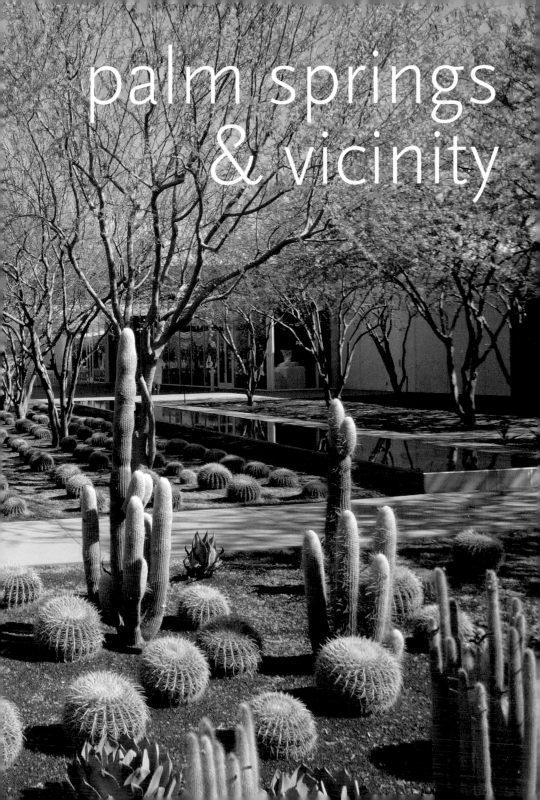

palm springs
& vicinity

joshua tree national park

74485 National Park Drive, Twentynine Palms, CA 92277
nps.gov/jotr
Visit February–April for cactus flowers and spring wildflower
season

- 📞 (760) 367-5500
- 🕐 Park open daily year-round 24 hours; visitor centers at
  north and south park entrances, at Oasis of Mara in
  Twentynine Palms, and at Black Rock campground are
  generally open 8am–5pm; check website for individual
  hours and locations
- $ Admission fee; park pass is good for 12 months and
  covers all passengers in a single vehicle
- 🐕 Dogs on leash

A national treasure, with spring-blooming wildflowers, unusual flora and fauna, and namesake Joshua trees

If you've been struck by the powerful beauty of cacti and other
desert plants in California gardens, consider an excursion to
Joshua Tree National Park. Located in the Little San Bernardino
Mountains about fifty miles northeast of Palm Springs (140 miles
east of Los Angeles), Joshua Tree provides a unique and unforgettable opportunity to get up close and personal with a vast desert
landscape and the different forms of plant and animal life it sup-
ports. I would strongly urge you to visit between February and
April, when many of the cacti and desert wildflowers are in bloom.
And I would just as strongly discourage you from visiting in the
summer when temperatures can soar to 110 degrees Fahrenheit.

Two great American deserts, the Colorado and the Mojave,
meet and overlap at Joshua Tree National Park. The park

Yucca brevifolia, the Joshua tree, grows in the higher elevations of the Mojave Desert in Joshua Tree National Park.

encompasses about 1,250 square miles, three-quarters of it designated wilderness. There are various drives and designated hikes and trails that will give you insights into the history, geology, animal life, and botanical wonders found in this forbidding and fragile world. If you're coming from Palm Springs, the easiest option is to begin at the west entrance and loop through the park to the Oasis of Mara at the north entrance. If you do that, give yourself at least three to four hours to stop, wonder, and explore.

This amazing landscape would not be a protected national park if it weren't for the tireless efforts of Minerva Hoyt (1866–1945), a Southern belle who became a passionate desert conservationist. Marriage took her from a plantation in Mississippi to a socialite's life in New York. Eventually she moved to Pasadena,

where she became an avid gardener at a time when cacti and desert plants were routinely used for home landscaping. Her passion was ignited when she saw firsthand the rampant destruction that was taking place in California's deserts. People were literally looting the landscape—uprooting and hauling away cacti and other native desert plants for their home gardens. After the death of her husband and son, Minerva channeled all her energies into raising awareness about the threatened desert landscapes. In 1936, after Minerva had crusaded for more than a decade to get California's deserts protected as national parks, President Roosevelt designated 825,000 acres of desert as the Joshua Tree National Monument. It received national park status in 1994.

An ocotillo in the starkly dramatic desert landscape at Joshua Tree National Park.

The western half of the park is the Mojave Desert. In this high desert, above 3,000 feet, you'll see the Joshua trees the park is named for. The trees are an unforgettable sight, reaching heights of 40 feet (at a growth rate of an inch per year) with thick trunks and upraised limbs that give them a muscular and at times tortured appearance. They were supposedly given their name by the Mormon soldiers who marched through the desert in 1846 on their way to wrest San Diego and all Alta California from Mexico. The Mormons likened the tree's outstretched branches to the strong, beckoning arms of Joshua, a Biblical figure who led the Israelites through the desert.

The Joshua tree is not a cactus, as many think, but a species of yucca (*Yucca brevifolia*) adapted to live at these higher elevations where six to eight inches of rain falls a year, and temperatures drop dramatically at night. Its thin, waxy leaves help it to conserve moisture in the parched summer months.

Over a dozen species of cacti make their home in the Mojave and the lower-elevation Colorado desert. Keep your eyes peeled and you'll encounter barrel cactus and prickly pear, botanical icons of the Old West, as well as hedgehog, foxtail, beavertail, and mound cactus. Seeing these ancient, spiny, hard-working plants in full vibrant bloom is what makes a visit to Joshua Tree such a memorable experience. The forms and the flowering patterns they have adapted to survive and reproduce is nothing short of amazing. Parry's nolina, for example, sends out a tall, feathery spray of blooms. The spiky leaves atop the Mojave yucca seem to hold aloft its thick white flower clusters. When conditions are right, red flowers open like flames on the tips of the many-branched ocotillo, drawing hummingbirds. Many such thin-stemmed and small-leaved shrubs and trees have also adapted to the harsh conditions of the Mojave. On the desert's rocky hillsides, gravelly slopes, sandy washes, and vast open flats, you'll see flowering shrubs like brittlebrush (*Encelia farinosa*); chuparosa (*Justicia californica*), with its multitude of red-orange flowers; yellow-flowering desert senna (*Senna armata*); and the lavender-hued Mojave aster (*Xylorhiza tortifolia*). Pinyon pines, junipers, scrub oaks, and ironwood trees also survive in parts of the park.

This hauntingly austere landscape, with its gigantic rock formations sculpted over eons by scorching desert winds, is home to a variety of birds, mammals, lizards, and insects, all marvelously adapted, like the plants, to the parched environment.

The Colorado Desert in the eastern half of the park is part of the much larger, and lower in elevation, Sonoran Desert. This huge, griddle-hot desert ecosystem in the Lower Colorado River Basin stretches across parts of Arizona and Mexico. The vegetation is different from the Mojave, dominated by creosote, ocotillo, and palo verde trees with their green trunks and leaves that turn bright yellow. If you visit the Cholla Cactus Garden, you'll see many different varieties of cholla. Don't get too close, though. The jumping cholla cactus got its name because it will hitch a ride on anyone or anything that brushes against it.

In the spring, eye-popping displays of wildflowers add brilliant daubs of color to the sere desert landscape. Flowering times for spring annuals can change from year to year, depending on winter precipitation and temperatures. The plants start blooming first in the lower elevations of the Colorado Desert, usually in February, around Pinto Basin and along the park's south boundary. Wildflowers may bloom as late as June in the higher elevations of the Mojave. Look for the brilliant orange-red mariposa lily (*Calochortus kennedyi*); the ghost flower (*Mohavea confertiflora*), its white petals sprinkled with reddish spots; the purple-blue stalks of Arizona lupine (*Lupinus arizonicus*); and the desert lily (*Hesperocallis undulata*), its tall stalk covered with striking white blossoms.

Thousands of years ago, after the glaciers of the last ice age receded, this environment was wetter and cooler than it is today. The people of the Pinto culture may have arrived more than 10,000 years ago. They and later native peoples lived on and near the Oasis of Mara, where underground springs allowed palm trees to flourish and other lush vegetation to grow. The life-giving waters of the oasis were channeled away by the miners, cattle ranchers, and homesteaders who began to arrive in the mid-nineteenth century, displacing the ancient native peoples of the desert. Their ruinous disregard for the fragile ecology of the desert led to the kind of wholesale destruction that moved Minerva Hoyt to take action back in the 1920s. In 2012, a mountain peak in the park was named Mount Minerva Hoyt, in her desert-loving honor.

On your trip to Joshua Tree, bring water, sunscreen, and a hat; there are no goods or services and limited facilities within the park. Some areas of the park are designated for day use only.

Moorten Botanical Garden

Cacti and desert plant aficionados in Palm Springs will enjoy a visit to Moorten Botanical Garden (1701 South Canyon Drive, Palm Springs, CA 92264; (760) 327-6555; admission fee; open Thurs–Tues 10am–4pm). The Moorten estate, called Desertland, is a one-of-a-kind relic of old Palm Springs, reminiscent of the home-grown attractions that once dotted America's highways. It was established in 1938 by Chester "Cactus Slim" Moorten and his wife Patricia. Slim Moorten, one of the original Keystone Kops of silent-film fame, moved to Palm Springs for his health. As the Moortens' interest in cacti and desert plants grew, they traveled throughout the Southwest and Baja deserts and down through Mexico to Guatemala, collecting specimens. Now their son Clark is the curator of this intriguing one-acre garden, where some 3,000 varieties of desert plants from throughout the world are arranged according to geographical region. There are some fascinating specimens to be seen outdoors and in the Cactarium (greenhouse). Interspersed with cacti, agaves, and other succulents are cardoon and boojum trees, petrified rocks, crystals, and desert memorabilia. If you're interested in bringing a thorny friend home with you, check out the plant nursery.

sunnylands center and gardens

A unique desert oasis created with today's drought-tolerant plants and sustainable gardening practices

37977 Bob Hope Drive, Rancho Mirage, CA 92270
sunnylands.org
Visit February–April for maximum blooms

....

- ☎ (769) 202-2222
- 🕐 Center and gardens open Thurs–Sun 8:30am–4pm; check website for exact dates (reserve far in advance to tour Annenberg estate)
- $ Center and gardens admission free; fee to tour Annenberg estate
- 🐕 No dogs

To showcase their dramatic forms and vivid colors, cacti and succulents are planted en masse at the new Sunnylands Center and Gardens.

The Annenberg fortune started with a racing form and a scandal. After Moe Annenberg, publisher of the *Daily Racing Form* and the *Philadelphia Inquirer*, got sent to prison for tax evasion, his son, Walter, sought to rehabilitate the family's name and lost fortunes. In 1942, Walter took over his father's failing business and turned it into a media giant that was eventually sold to Rupert Murdoch for $3 billion. Along the way, besides starting *TV Guide* and *Seventeen* magazines, Walter Annenberg collected art; hobnobbed with presidents, royalty, and celebrities; became U.S. ambassador to Great Britain; and turned his attention to philanthropy and public service. I mention all this because Sunnylands Center and Gardens is part of the Annenberg estate and wouldn't exist without Annenberg money. It's a wonderful garden to visit. Not only is it a beautifully unique desert garden, it was created with today's sustainable gardening and building practices in mind. It's not often that we get to enjoy a contemporary public garden of this caliber—and at no charge.

Sunnylands, Walter and Leonore Annenberg's 202-acre estate in Rancho Mirage, is sometimes called the Camp David of the West because of all the presidents and heads of state who were guests there. The Annenbergs built their 22,000-square-foot mid-century modern house in 1966 and wintered there for the next thirty-three years. The interiors were done by Billy Haines, Hollywood's first openly gay actor who later became decorator to the stars. Annenberg's billion-dollar collection of French Impressionist works hung on the walls (they now hang in the Metropolitan Museum in New York). Frank Sinatra sang at the Annenbergs' soirees, Bob Hope emceed, and a constant stream of guests drawn from the worlds of politics, royalty, and entertainment enjoyed the lavish hospitality of Sunnylands. The Annenbergs were so rich and so exacting that one person was hired just to replace broken potato chips in a bowl in the guest wing. Much of the outdoor space was a private nine-hole golf course. When the grass turned brown—as grass tends to do in the desert—it was painted green so as not to cause offense. You can visit their house if you book a tour months in advance. Touring the grounds of the estate via an open minivan is easier and less expensive. Although Sunnylands' golf course landscaping is mighty boring, you'll get a glimpse of the house where the soirees were legendary because of the legends that partied there.

But you don't need to do any of that, really, because the new Sunnylands Center and Gardens are the most enjoyable part of a visit to Sunnylands—for garden lovers, anyway. Spend an hour or two exploring the garden, then maybe have lunch, coffee, or a glass of wine in the café.

The center, which opened in 2012, is like an updated version of the midcentury modern style of the Annenbergs' palatial home. It's meant to interpret and promote the Annenberg legacy and largesse. Your first view of the nine-acre garden that surrounds the center is, according to landscape designer James Burnett, an homage to Van Gogh's 1889 painting *Olive Trees*, a work once owned by Walter Annenberg. The bright yellow flowers of palo verde trees (*Parkinsonia* 'Desert Museum') border a circular green lawn beyond a blue reflecting pool, with the San Jacinto Mountains in the distance—all making for a brilliant composition.

The parklike garden draws you in and captures your attention at every turn. The first beds are single-species plantings of cacti and other desert plants. Rows of spiny golden barrel cacti, beaked yuccas, and thorn-tipped aloes and agaves lined up with military precision may not be everyone's idea of a garden, but the effect is striking and draws attention to the sculptural form of desert plants. Many of the cacti and succulents grow in the dappled

Fallen leaves and flowers from palo verde trees add a sweep of yellow to the beds at Sunnylands Center and Gardens.

shade of the palo verde trees, which drop their bright yellow flowers and leaves among the greens, blues, and grays of the succulents. And in the spring, when red-flowered ocotillos bloom and the yuccas, aloes, and agaves send up their flower stalks, still more color is added.

There's a restful, even contemplative aspect to the garden behind the center. It encloses you in an environment with many quietly inviting spots to sit and enjoy the plantings and the birds and butterflies they attract. On one side of the Great Lawn, a labyrinth enlivened by trailing smokebush (*Dalea greggii*) acts as a meditation circle, its design based on similar labyrinths found in medieval European cathedrals. The twin reflecting pools filled with stones are another contemplative feature in the gardens behind the center.

Low-water plants and shrubs were used to create the new gardens at Sunnylands, a part of the Annenberg estate in Rancho Mirage

The gardens continue in front, on both sides of the drive from the main entrance to the parking lot. Don't let your initial drive-through suffice; take a meandering path and enjoy these spaces and the plants in them up close. One side of the driveway is almost entirely taken up by a wildflower meadow. Here, starting in February, you'll be treated to an ongoing display of arid-environment beauties. Impressionist works formed a backdrop to the Annenbergs' life at Sunnylands, and re-creating in nature the paintings' shimmering beauty is an underlying theme of the garden. When you see the meadow with its flowering sages, verbenas, desert marigolds, daisies, and poppies, you might be tempted to take up a paintbrush yourself.

A trio of topiary mariachi players greets visitors at the San Diego Botanic Garden in Encinitas.

san diego & vicinity

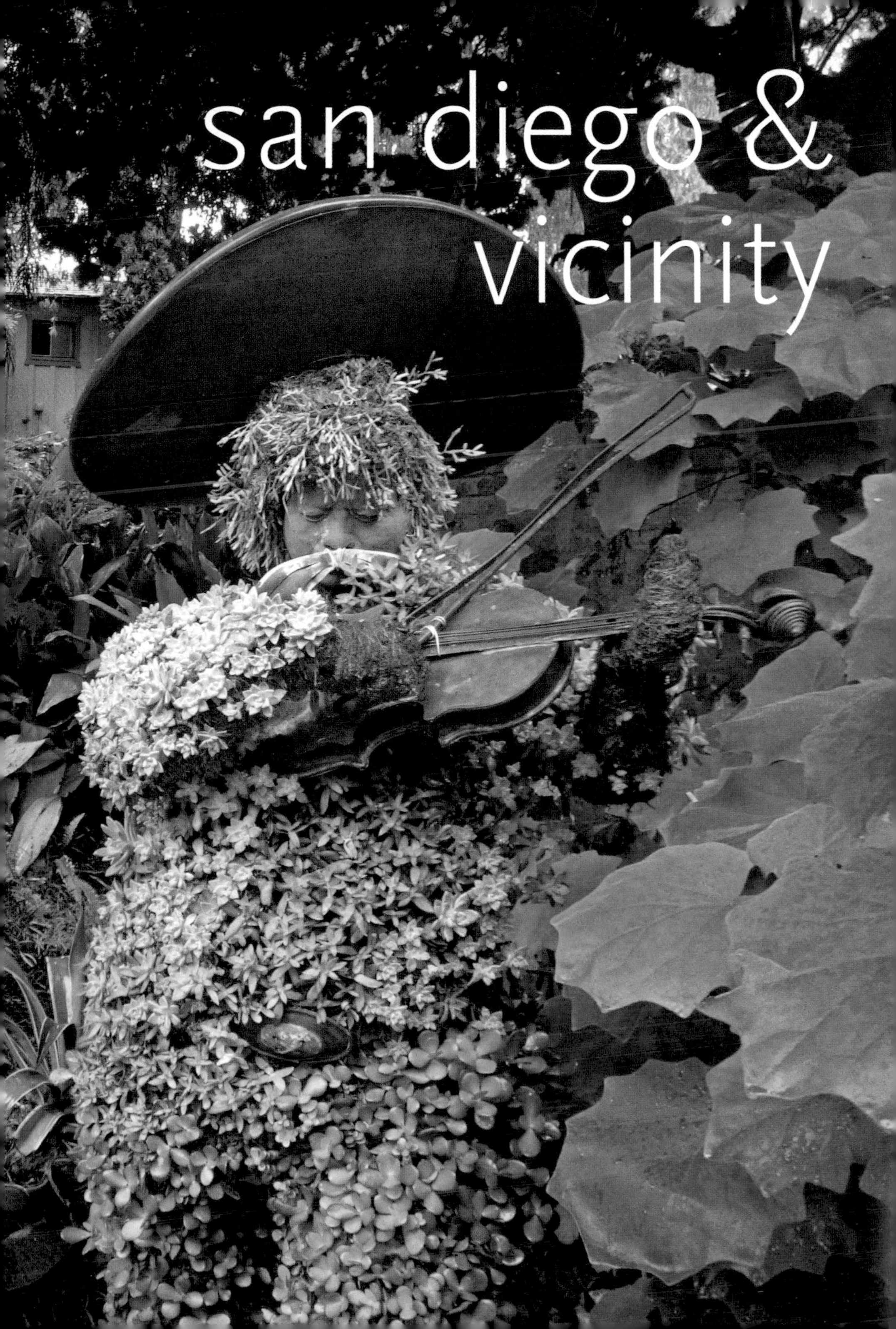

balboa park

1549 El Prado, San Diego, CA 92101
balboapark.org
Visit year-round; Rose Garden in bloom April–September;
   Desert Garden January–March

- 📞 (619) 239-0512
- 🕐 Park gardens open daily year-round; visitor center
  open daily 9:30am–4:30pm; Botanical Building closed
  Thursdays and holidays; Japanese Friendship Garden
  open daily 10am–4pm
- 💲 Admission free; admission fee for Japanese Friendship
  Garden and museums; check website for available tours
- 🚌 Public transportation
- 🐕 Dogs on leash

Nineteen gardens in an outstanding city park that once housed a professional nudist colony

You'd need at least a week to explore everything in this giant park—larger than Central Park and considered the cultural heart of San Diego—but you can visit the most significant gardens in half a day or less. Before we get to the gardens, and the nudist colony, however, a little history is in order. The land that is now Balboa Park—all 1,400 acres of it—was set aside as parkland in 1868, when the population of San Diego was about 2,300 (today it's over 1.3 million). Nothing much was done with the land until 1902, when landscape architect Samuel Parsons was hired to create a plan for what was then called City Park. Parsons, who was the head landscape architect for New York City, had been an assistant and then partner of Calvert Vaux, co-designer with Frederick Olmsted of New York's Central Park. Like Vaux and Olmsted, Parsons favored naturalistic parks adorned with Beaux-Arts architectural elements. But unlike the parks Parsons had worked on in New York, which were designed to block out the

Built for the 1915 Panama-California Exposition and home to over 2,000 tropical plants, the Botanical Building in Balboa Park is sheathed with strips of redwood and fronted by the beautiful Lily Pond.

city around them, Balboa Park was designed to look outward, toward the mesas and Pacific Ocean that were an integral part of the natural landscape. Before the advent of high-rises that blocked the ocean views, Balboa Park did just that. Like the views, many of Parsons's early plantings are gone now, but much of his overall scheme remains. One other person has to be mentioned in connection with the creation of Balboa Park and its plant collections: the indefatigable Kate Sessions (1857–1940). Sometimes called the Mother of Balboa Park, the San Francisco–born Sessions persuaded the (male) powers that be to hire Parsons as landscape designer. She worked out a deal with the city to act as the park's horticulturist, supplying plants and supervising plantings. She did all this in an era when women still didn't have the right to vote, and continued to do so until her death.

The walled Alcazar Garden in Balboa Park was created for the 1935 World's Fair.

In 1910, the park was renamed Balboa Park after Vasco Núñez de Balboa, the first European to see the Pacific Ocean (no matter that the area's Kumeyaay people had been looking at the same ocean for at least 10,000 years). San Diego, like all West Coast cities at the time, was eager to publicize itself and boost its growth. When it lost a bid to be the official site of the 1915 World's Fair (to San Francisco), it held a fair of its own, the vastly successful Panama-California Exposition. Many of the park's Spanish Colonial Revival buildings date from that time. They were put up quickly, almost like stage sets, and weren't meant to be permanent. But they're still there, preserved and protected, and add immeasurably to the park's unique historical character. One strikingly beautiful structure from that era is the Botanical Building, a graceful steel and cast-iron conservatory sheathed with strips of redwood lath and fronted by the long, rectangular Lily Pond, which is planted with waterlilies. The building shelters a collection of over 2,000 tropical plants, including carnivorous flytraps and dinosaur-era cycads. The Japanese Friendship Garden, among the oldest Japanese-style gardens in the United States, also dates from the 1915 exposition. The first palms in the park's Palm Canyon were planted around that time. Twenty years later, in 1935, San Diego finally got its wish and was chosen as the site of the official U.S. World's Fair, called the California Pacific International Exposition. Again, Balboa Park was the focus of activity. More buildings went up and more gardens were built, including the lovely Alcazar Garden, a walled garden inspired by the courtyard gardens at Alcazar Castle in Seville, Spain, with fountains and formal boxwood parterres planted with colorful annuals.

Here's where the nudist colony makes its appearance. An especially titillating attraction at the 1935 fair was a colony of so-called professional nudists who lived behind a high fence in the Zoro Garden. Today this sunken garden with its rock walls and winding paths is planted as a butterfly garden and used for (fully clothed) performances of Shakespeare plays. Back in 1935, however, it was the nudists who performed: you could pay to look through a peephole in the fence and watch them cavorting au naturel. For that same 1935 fair, Kate Sessions designed the Cactus Garden, located behind the Balboa Park Club. Though it doesn't compare to the jaw-dropping collections you can see at Lotusland or the Huntington Library gardens, it's worth seeking out—and not much visited because it's off the beaten track. Just north of it is the

Casa del Rey Moro (House of the Moorish Kings) Gardens, also from the 1935 fair. A plaza garden with a fountain, it re-creates the Moorish gardens that the garden designer, Richard Requa, visited in Rondo, Spain. All these historic gardens are close to the park's giant central plaza, as is Palm Canyon, another must-see. A wooden staircase takes you down into the canyon, home to over sixty species of mature palms from around the world. As you head down, you'll pass the enormous roots of a towering Moreton Bay fig (*Ficus macrophylla*), a famous specimen tree in the park; the tallest palms are the Mexican fan palms, now over ninety years old.

There are two gardens east of Park Boulevard that you may also want to visit. The first is the Inez Grant Parker Memorial Rose Garden, an All-America Rose Selections garden loaded with over 1,600 roses that bloom from April through September. More interesting is the adjacent garden which looks out over the Florida Canyon Native Plant Preserve, an undeveloped canyon with representative species of San Diego's native flora. The plants in the Desert Garden—winter-blooming cacti, aloes, agaves, and euphorbias—are living memories of the 1935 fair. They were first planted where the Cactus Garden is today and moved to this location in 1976. But older still is the coastal sage scrub and southern maritime chaparral below and across the canyon. That's what the land looked like long before Samuel Parsons and Kate Sessions transformed Balboa Park into the botanical showcase it is today.

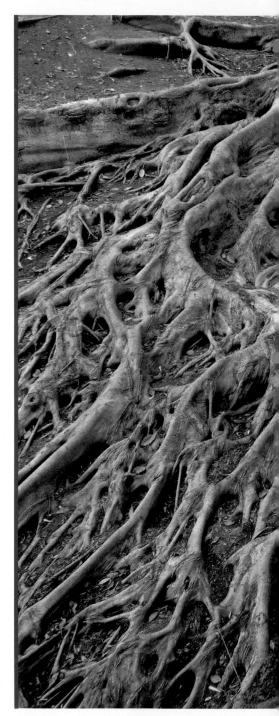

Heading into Palm Canyon at Balboa Park, you'll pass the massive roots of a towering Moreton Bay fig.

san diego botanic garden

Home to rare and endangered plants from around the world, including an acclaimed cycad collection

230 Quail Gardens Drive, Encinitas, CA 92023
sdbgarden.org
Visit year-round; cacti and aloes bloom January–March

....

📞 (760) 436-3036
🕐 Open daily 9am–5pm; closed Dec 25
$ Admission fee
🐕 No dogs

Until fairly recently, the area around Encinitas was known as the Flower Capital of the World. Every spring, vast fields of ranunculus spread a carpet of color as far as the eye could see. In the 1960s, the area became an epicenter for the mass production of poinsettias. The ranunculus fields are mostly gone now, replaced by housing developments and stores, and the poinsettia industry has moved to Honduras, but tucked into this increasingly urbanized landscape, about twenty-six miles north of downtown San Diego, is the San Diego Botanic Garden, thirty-seven acres of pleasure for plant lovers.

Ruth Baird Larabee, who purchased the oceanview property in 1942 and eventually bequeathed it to San Diego County for use as a public park, was married to Charles Larabee, her childhood sweetheart. Both Ruth and Charles inherited private fortunes, but you'd never know it from the modest cottage they built, which now serves as a research library and interpretive center. The Larabees were avid outdoorspeople and plant lovers, though Ruth, a Vassar graduate, seems to have been the one who started the gardens. She was also interested in land conservation, and part of her rationale for bequeathing this property to the county was to preserve habitat for the native quail population. In fact, up until 2009, the garden was known as Quail Botanical Gardens, and many locals still call it that.

Rare and sumptuous as many of the plants in this garden are, the eight acres of undeveloped coastal sage scrub and southern maritime chaparral are rarer still. This is what much of the coastline still looked like when the Larabees arrived in 1942; in the ensuing decades, as San Diego has developed, redeveloped, and overdeveloped, native habitat has shrunk to a tiny fraction of its original size. That's why I recommend beginning your tour at the Native Plants and Native People Trail. This isn't a showy landscape, but it's pure California, with plants that are tough, hardy,

The giant flower of Brazilian Dutchman's pipe (*Aristolochia gigantea*), aka duckflower, stops visitors to the San Diego Botanic Garden in their tracks.

drought resistant, low to the ground, and accustomed to wildfires. The semi-deciduous coastal sage scrub plants include buckwheat, black sage, and California sagebrush, while the shrubby southern maritime chaparral plants—chamise, scrub oaks, and now-endangered Del Mar manzanitas—are evergreen. There's also a riparian wetlands area with tules, rushes, and willows. The Kumeyaay people who inhabited this coastline at least 10,000 years ago used many of these plants for food, medicine, making baskets, and building shelters. The native plants and the reproduction of a native homesite were blessed by one of the last Kumeyaay natives to speak the language.

Have a look, too, at the Fire Safety Garden and landscaping display just south of the Native Plants Trail. It's an excellent source of fire-savvy planting ideas suited for San Diego's hot, dry, wildfire-prone summers. The area south of the parking lot is also where you'll find the Eucalyptus Grove with wonderfully scented lemon gums (*Corymbia citriodora*). Contrary to popular belief, eucalyptus trees are native to Australia, not California. These eucalyptus were planted by the Larabees and are the oldest trees in the garden.

Plants like *Portea petropolitana* and *Cordyline fruticosa* 'Red Sister' add brilliant color to the lower pond in the Tropical Rain Forest at the San Diego Botanic Garden.

The map you get at the admission booth provides a self-guided trail loop that will take you through the many specialty gardens and collections north and west of the parking lot. Give yourself at least ninety minutes to enjoy a leisurely stroll; there are many places where you'll want to stop and gawk. The collections are arranged by geographical area. Besides the eucalyptus, there are three rare tree collections in this garden that are worth seeking out. In the Canary Islands Garden there's a stunning grove of dragon blood trees (*Dracaena cinnabari*), native to the Socotra Archipelago in the Indian Ocean. The name comes from the tree's red sap, which Stradivarius and Amati used as a resin to coat their famous violins. These beautiful trees, with their densely packed, umbrella-shaped crowns, are now threatened in their native habitat because of lower humidity and moisture rates brought on by climate change. In the California Natives planting, you'll find rare Torrey pines (*Pinus torreyana*), a graceful tree whose range is limited to the Channel Islands and Torrey Pines State Natural Reserve in La Jolla. There are also mature specimens of cork oaks (*Quercus suber*), an evergreen tree native to southwestern Europe and northwestern Africa and used to make wine corks and cork flooring.

The San Diego Botanic Garden is also renowned for its cycad collection. With over 140 varieties, it's among the largest cycad collections in the world, rivaled in California only by the magnificent collection at Lotusland. If you've never encountered these primitive beauties whose ancestors hark back to the Triassic and Jurassic age of the dinosaurs, here's your chance. Dramatic-looking plants, with stout, woody trunks and stiff crowns of palmlike leaves, cycads are prized by collectors and often unscrupulously obtained. That's why they are increasingly rare, threatened, and even extinct in their native African and Mexican habitats. The San Diego Botanic Garden obtained several of its cycads because it's a rescue garden for rare and stolen plants confiscated by state and federal authorities. They couldn't have a nicer home away from home.

The garden recently expanded the Hamilton Children's Garden, so if you have kids or grandkids, be sure to bring them along. They'll be able to dig in the dirt, play in a treehouse made out of living banyan roots, watch native quail, chase butterflies, and generally have a ball. So will you.

acknowledgments

This book could not have been written without the behind-the-wheel and behind-the-computer help of Gary Larson and Tim Kirkpatrick. Special thanks go to Tom Fischer, Julie Talbot, Sarah Milhollin, Franni Farrell, and all the folks at Timber Press who helped this project along. I am also indebted to all the directors and docents who shared their knowledge and shepherded me around their wonderful gardens.

photo credits

index

about the author

Donald Olson is a travel writer, novelist, playwright, and author of *The Pacific Northwest Garden Tour*, also published by Timber Press. His travel stories have appeared in the *New York Times*, *National Geographic*, and other national publications. He has written many city and country guides, including *England for Dummies*, *London for Dummies*, and *Germany for Dummies*, and more recently, the Frommer's guides *Portland Day by Day*, *Seattle Day by Day*, *Berlin Day by Day*, and *Frommer's EasyGuide to Seattle, Portland, and the Oregon Coast*. An avid gardener, Donald has been exploring and photographing the great gardens of Europe and the United States for many years, and gardens have played prominent roles in his fiction (*Paradise Gardens*) and plays (*The Garden Plays*). His most recent novels were published under the pen name Swan Adamson. Donald lives, writes, and gardens in Manhattan and in Portland, Oregon. Visit him at donaldstevenolson.com and on Facebook.

TIM KIRKPATRICK